COACH GOD

THE MYSTERY OF THE GAME PLAN

Joseph Lovett

ISBN 978-1-64300-326-9 (Paperback)
ISBN 978-1-64300-327-6 (Digital)

Covenant Books, Inc.
11661 Hwy 707
Murrells Inlet, SC 29576
www.covenantbooks.com

In memory of Carol "Gram" Christian LaPointe

I asked her to be one of my readers, but she was too sick to read it.
As Thomas A. Kempis said in *The Imitation of Christ*, when we die,
"We will not be asked what we have read, but what we have done."
Like our best coaches and in imitation of Coach
God, she believed we were that good until we were
that good. Thanks for everything, Gram!

It is a beautiful book and promises to help many people. Sports are a blessing to those who are passionate and thoughtful about their value and teachings. Thank you for including my spiritual journey.

—Nancy Frates

I really appreciate how Joe captures so vividly the events that took place 15 years ago and remain a part of my DNA as an adult. For me personally and as I've grown older, the Division 1 Massachusetts Super Bowl in 2002 really serves as a microcosm of life; we all experience loss throughout our respective journeys, are humbled by those losses and are ultimately empowered with the choice of how we respond to them. I know that along my journey and in experiencing different losses outside of sport, I've developed a strong sense of awareness of how important it is to really embrace and grieve in those moments. And as loss is an experience that inevitably we all share I've learned to hold deeper empathy for those around me at all times and a greater appreciation for what it takes to carry one another through real adversity. We all have an opportunity to be a positive force for someone navigating the emotions of loss, and I am eternally grateful for the support that Joe provided me following that game in 2002.

—Steven Van Note, Class of '03

I made my way through Coach God earlier this summer and it was a wonderfully written, thought-provoking, enjoyable read. I am honored to have been mentioned and I look forward to its publishing. I will certainly be picking up a copy.

–Steven D. Langton
Olympic Medalist & World Champion
United States Olympic Team '10 '14 '18

CONTENTS

FOREWORD

I am a product of sixteen years of Catholic education: first at St. Agnes School in Arlington, Massachusetts, followed by four years at St. Johns Preparatory School, concluding with four years at the University of Notre Dame. The decision on the first two schools was made by my parents. I chose Notre Dame after my official visit; it felt like St. John's Prep on steroids. I am also the product of twenty years of organized sports. That decision was made by my parents too but took very little convincing once I got started. I loved the competition and was blessed with size and athleticism. I worked to get better because it was something I wasn't willing to give up. It paid off and I am a professional athlete, but it was more than hard work that got me there.

This book tells my story of a life of sports and spirituality. I experienced all the successes and failures that Coach Lovett writes about in these pages. I prayed for foul shots to go in and fastballs to go over the plate. I prayed for the answers on Latin tests and math quizzes. I prayed for Jared and Brandon Coppola and everyone in their family. Were all my prayers answered? Certainly not. But a lot of good things happened when I kept praying.

I am grateful to have been coached by men like Joe Lovett, John Barbati, and Bill Britton. They taught us the right way to play the game, to win with class, and lose with grace. Although losing was never a consideration, it was very infrequently a reality. They taught us so much more than sports. Their message was to live life with a moral compass and to have humility and compassion. To be Christian. We were never required to wear our religion on our sleeve. We were only expected to become men in every sense of the word. I am quite sure if Brian St. Pierre or Chris Zardas or any of the athletes mentioned in the following pages were writing this foreword, the story would be the same.

There are 450 people in the world who play basketball at the highest level. I worked to achieve what was truly a dream. There were many things that went right for me in my journey. I don't believe it was luck or being in the right place at the right time. I know I have a responsibility to use my celebrity as a professional athlete for the benefit of others. That's a good thing. I feel that responsibility because I am the product of an environment that teaches service to the less fortunate.

Coach God has put me in the game; I don't intend to let him down.

Pat Connaughton

ACKNOWLEDGMENTS

"Come, Holy Spirit, fill the hearts of the faithful and enkindle in them the fire of your love. Send forth your spirit and we shall be created, and thou shalt renew the face of the earth. O God, who by the light of the Holy Spirit, dost instruct the hearts of the faithful, grant that by the same Spirit, we may be truly wise and ever rejoice in its consolation." The Very Reverend Father Mullaney, OP. uttered this prayer before every graduate-school Christology class. He was the humblest man I have ever met and strengthened my faith in the reality of Jesus and God's presence in our lives just by reading the scriptures. Throughout this work, I have had numerous, very sacred encounters with people more than willing to share their personal stories of their spiritual journey, and I attribute that to the work of the Spirit helping us to find God's wisdom in sports. I thank the Holy Spirit and Very Reverend Father Mullaney, OP, for introducing me to the Holy Spirit.

I would like to thank my wife Diane for supporting me in this work even though it was hard for her to share my enthusiasm as her mother was dying throughout its writing. I also thank my entire family: my daughter Jennifer, son Sean, and my faithful companion, Keeper, who lay right behind me as I wrote until the day he died. My parents, Tom and Laura, together with my sister Terri, listened patiently each weekend as I shared the progress of the book. In a special way, I thank Carol Christian LaPointe (deceased) and the entire LaPointe family for accepting me despite my sense of humor.

Author Brendan Kiely gave me the courage to share my voice with the readers. It was my meeting with him that gave me hope someone might publish and read what I had to say. Editors Eli (ND Press) and Jon Sweeney (Ave Maria Press) went out of their way to help the work get published even though it was not in their self-interest to do so. My readers, Lawrence Molloy, Peter Dankert, and Sean Sennott all offered invaluable insight and kept me on track, being true to my voice. Susan Bavaro and Raisa Carrasco-Velez welcomed me into their offices unannounced to sit down and share the newest developments in the book. A special thanks to Kasha Foret and Kris Kempinski and the entire Covenant Books family who helped turn my vision for the book into reality. They made everything exceedingly easy!

Thanks to all of those wonderful people who sat with me and allowed me to listen to their extraordinary stories of faith. These were truly grace-filled moments. I hope I have honored Nancy and Peter Frates, Dawn and Jared Coppola, Pat Connaughton, Mark Bavaro, Bryan Nju-Ghong, John Barbati, and Bill "Will" Britton. I especially appreciate Pat Connaughton's faith-filled Foreword that he, and his father Leonard, so humbly provided for the book.

I am grateful to the administrators of Trinity High School and St. John's Preparatory School who gave me the opportunity to meet, teach, and coach all the athletes in the book. I especially thank Jim O'Leary, the athletic director and camp director at St. John's Prep, for putting me in positions of coaching and camp administration that enabled me to experience God's grace by meeting so many wonderful people through sports. Dan Riley, Chris Zardas, Dan Mullen, Steve Langton, Steve Van Note, Chip Schreunder, and Shannon Fish have all impacted my life in numerous positive ways, sometimes without even knowing. I also would like to thank the coaches I have worked with who lent their wisdom to the contents of the book, including Brian St. Pierre, Ray Carey, Sean Connolly, Jack Klein, John Boyle, Bill Boyle, Derek Journeay, Dana Smith, Steve Clifford, John Roy, Peter Argeros, and Dave McHenry. I thank the Xaverian Brothers who live their mission every day and encouraged me to find God in the "ordinary, unspectacular flow of everyday life." I would like to thank everyone who has forgiven me for the times I have not been the coach God would have wanted me to be, including Ulyen Coleman. Sometimes it takes years and to realize how much better I could have been.

Lastly, I would like to thank Mary, the mother of Jesus. Her presence was palpable throughout the writing of the book in the lives of many of my interviewees, especially as they lived the mystery of suffering in life. Like many a spouse of coaches, she is really the source of strength behind the scenes. She is the quiet strength of many successful athletic works, as she was for this book. Thanks, Mom!

INTRODUCTION
TAKE A KNEE

When youngsters start playing organized sports, their parents exhort them to have fun, to look at and listen to the coach when the coach is talking. As players, we all remember taking a knee or sitting on a bench doing just that while our parents patiently waited to pick us up from practice or a game. Our sporting lives are not separate from our spiritual lives. Through sports, our head coach, Coach God, instructs us if we are but willing to take spiritual postures of humility and faith. Coach God empowers assistant coaches—namely parents, fellow players, and even actual coaches—to teach us what we need to hear. God loves us. God is with us, even when we fail or lose. As our best coach ever, Coach God believes that we will be that good until we are that good. From conception on, we are always in the game, discerning and living out the game plan for us and others. Through practice in virtues, we grow closer to teammates and our coaches. Together we live out the mystery of that game plan. We just need to take a knee and look and listen.

I first started listening to Coach God as a young coach in the 1980s. "I really hope I can clear that height," Michelle said to me at the indoor state track meet in 1987.

"Maybe you should pray," I suggested. Lo and behold, Michelle cleared the height, a personal best, on her third and final attempt. When she came over brimming with excitement, I shared her enthusiasm and asked, "So did you pray?"

Her answer has stayed with me all of these years. "No, Coach, I didn't. I figured God cares about me even when I don't pray!"

I couldn't agree more. God loves all of us all the time. He has given us sports to reveal to us so much about ourselves, our relationships with others, and our love relationship with God. God wants us to pursue excellence, to risk, and to try to become our very best. We strive, we suffer, and we fail (as Michelle did at the next height). Through it all, our coach is with us, perfecting us, lifting us up when we fail, and encouraging us.

This book is a collection of my reflections on thirty-four years of coaching high school sports as a religious studies teacher and the impact on the spiritual lives of that journey on myself, my family, my colleagues, and some of the best athletes and people in the world. But most of all, it is about the one who makes all of our spiritual growth through sports possible. I am only an assistant coach in the same way that our earthly parents brought us into existence in cooperation with God's spirit. This book is about the ultimate teacher or coach, a person I have come to know as Coach God.

I have coached varsity high school sports for thirty-four years. During that time, I have had the privilege to accompany many men and women on their journey of faith. I have been fortunate to coach in Catholic schools where prayer is encouraged in all aspects of life. I can remember John Roy as an assistant basketball coach praying the Hail Mary before games with the team and ending with an emphatic "Our Lady of Victory, pray for us!" I wonder what had led him to believe that Mary had a role in the outcome of a high school basketball game. I still lead our football team in the Our Father before we go out to games. Each year, indeed each game, it takes on varied meanings. This prayer that unites all Christians is so rich that each of us can derive meaning in our own way each time it is uttered. Sometimes I pray as a petitioner for a suffering teammate, sometimes I feel like giving praise to God, and other times I just ask for whatever the players need. I always pray for health. It took writing this book to realize I should stick with "Your will be done" as my most constant (and most difficult) prayer. I don't know what each person in that room needs. I just pray and hope that God will bless them with whatever that need is, and then I go coach as if our opponents need to lose. Our head coach used to always say he respected anyone who put on the pads and snapped on the helmets to play such a violent, demanding game. But does God want them to play? Some youths only play for their parents.

I never wanted my son to play at a young age. In third grade, I came home from practice. My wife said, "We have a problem. Your son does not want to play football."

I went upstairs and opened the door only to be greeted with, "Blah, blah, blah. I know you want me to play football."

I sat on his bed and said, "I don't care if you are the tuba player in the band. I'll watch you at halftime. Find something you love and do it."

When I came home from my practice when he was in fifth grade, I went upstairs to tuck him in and asked about his first day of football practice. "Good", he said, "I really like to nail people."

I queried, "And how do you feel about getting hit?"

"I like that too," he said.

I told him that he should play a contact sport, like football, hockey, or rugby. But rugby scared me. I wasn't getting up for early hockey practices so I guess football it was if he wanted to hit people. But these are not the only contact sports. I have come to believe that all sports are contact sports; i.e., points of contact with God as we integrate our faith into our lives. Some claim sports are as much a religion as Christianity used to be.

For many people, Sundays have become more of an occasion for morning practices, pregame tailgates, and golf outings than an occasion to worship in sacred space. Sports come replete with their own set of rituals, traditions, and symbols, and some considered their arenas hallowed ground. Choosing sports over the sacred is not an either-or dichotomous proposition. Nothing could be further from the truth! Our spiritual and sporting lives are intimately intertwined together in reality. I do believe Sunday mornings should be reserved for gathering as a community in sacred space to let the symbols, words, and rituals of our liturgical life speak to us. These moments of grace in encountering Jesus in the Eucharist nurture our spiritual life and strengthen us for our spiritual journeys. However, I also believe that when we pause on the Sabbath (or throughout the week) to contemplate our daily vocations as parents, players, and coaches, Coach God challenges us to enter more fully into the mystery of the game plan.

The Daughter of Man

My daughter is the best! Or maybe it is my son. Anyway, they must be the best because I am their coach. That means I can put them in the positions in youth sports where they are the star players. They should be the point guard, the pitcher, or the quarterback. They can get all the reps in practice, all the glory, all the press, and all of the opportunities. This drives me crazy in youth sports.

As a high school coach, I have coached three decades of football and basketball and two decades of track and field. But I have also been asked to assist in youth basketball, baseball, and softball. The children's youth programs needed moms and dads to volunteer so that our children can have the opportunity to learn what Coach God wants us to learn through sports. That is not only true for me, but for moms and dads across our country. In a sense, many of us are going to be responsible for the spiritual formation of children as a sacred trust. Sometimes we may not even know much about the sport itself. (I was actually scared of the ball in baseball and studied it for three years until I felt competent to help coach little league.) But based on how God has instructed us, I think we can do a great job if we look at how God treated the Son of Man.

I am a Christian, but I have been welcomed into the Jewish family as a Holocaust Legacy Partner. I also have profound respect for my Hindu and Muslim students. I will admit that most of my learning about Coach God has come through a Christian lens. Through that lens, I believe that Coach God is the anti-nepotist. God sent his only son not to be served, but to serve. Jesus was like the scout team player that sacrifices the health of his body every single day to execute another team's offense so that the starters can be successful on game day. Jesus is like Jason Larocque, former bullpen catcher for the Boston Red Sox and now an associate principal of a middle school. He never saw the field or received ovations from the fans at Fenway but sacrificed to prepare his teammates to be their best. Now he volunteers in his hometown to educate coaches as a Little League board member. They are lucky to have him lead them in this way! In New England, many fans deify Coach Bill Belichick, but he isn't far off from how God asked Jesus to live his life when he instilled his "Do your job" attitude in his players and organization. Everyone has a role in executing Coach God's game plan. In each role we are called to "Be perfect as your heavenly Father is perfect." His humility and self-sacrifice not only taught us what it means to be fully human, but to be the ultimate team player. Not blaming others for failures, but overcoming perceived failures to bring new life to a situation and to others.

I have had students ask me if I think most coaches see through a Christian lens, but I can only speak from my own experience and what I have read. I grew up reading books like *I Am Third* by Gale Sayers and about the fellowship of Christian athletes. I was on the sidelines and in the huddle when I was five and would hear my coaching father thank the "Good Man Upstairs" with his team after each game. The first time I heard this, I was so young. I actually wondered who was living upstairs from us. But it stuck with me. After games, we should give thanks for the opportunity, the physical ability, the spiritual straining, and the fellowship. The image of Jesus responding to Coach God's call to self-sacrifice makes sense. So do Eucharistic team meals, post-game tailgates, prayer services, and team reunions.

Having a daughter who is an athlete has changed my perspective somewhat. As a Catholic, I had to overcome the inherent sexism in the institution, scriptural scholarship, and liturgical language of the church. Hence, the daughter of man works as well for me in understanding how Coach God works with athletes. When my daughter was ten, she had an 8:30 a.m. Amateur Athletic Union (AAU) basketball game one and one half hours away from our home. She played for two minutes the entire game. I was her coach. According to my assistant coach, the parents in the stands were asking, "What is wrong with Coach Lovett? Why isn't he playing his daughter?" Apparently, my daughter was wondering also as she was privately complaining to my wife throughout the day. My wife Diane actually responded to Jennifer as I would hope all parents would respond when athletes complain about their coaches. She told her to ask me. So while I was grilling some hamburgers that night, she came out to our deck and asked, "How come you only played me two minutes?"

I said, "You had seven turnovers in eight possessions. We won by one. Do you think we were going to lose the game just because you are my daughter? If you want to play, work harder and get better." I love my daughter. We both love basketball and spent many years going to the gym together to work on her game. But what would I have been teaching her if I kept her in as point guard regardless of her performance? What would her teammates be learning? One doesn't have to work because one is the coach's daughter? One should just automatically play the most in the most prominent position and the success of the team is contingent on your performance? I do not believe this is how Coach God wants us to love our daughters and sons. This is not how God dealt with his only Son. God sent his Son so that we might have life and have it abundantly, not to show the world how great his Son was. He learned obedience even unto death on a cross, the ultimate self-sacrifice. I have not coached my daughter very often so she also had to learn obedience to her coaches who are not her father.

Since my son plays football, I taught him to do everything his coach tells him unless it is unethical, like trying to intentionally hurt a player or under no circumstances was he to tackle with his head down. I did not want him paralyzed or killed playing a contact sport by being taught something more dangerous than the sport is ordinarily. My daughter encountered her own challenge with obedience to the coach in a good way. During her junior year of field hockey, her head coach and the captains were looking for an underclass player to become the field hockey goalie after the senior goalie's graduation. My wife was opposed because my daughter loves to run. As a matter of fact, she and I would blast and belt out "Born to Run" by Bruce Springsteen as we drove home from every athletic contest. It has become emblematic of our father-daughter relationship. She was insistent that she would not be the goalie. I reminded her that she would do whatever the coach asked of her. That was her responsibility as a player and teammate. Players don't get to choose their roles. They accept their role with humility and obedience. The daughter of man, like the Son of Man. In doing so, she was doing something Christlike, self-sacrificing what was asked of her for the good of all. She embraced the role, albeit begrudgingly. She worked out in the summer with a collegiate goalie to work on her skills. She came to understand that goalies are tremendous athletes with good hands, good feet, and an iron will. That will has to be used for the team, not for the individual, even though the success of goalies is often measured by individual statistics. She ended up quarterbacking the defense for two years, and I believe it made her not only a better teammate, but also a better person. She is playing neither field hockey nor basketball anymore. She plays lacrosse for Wheaton College in Massachusetts, which is the sport I thought she had the most talent for all along. (I bribed her with ice cream to pick up a lacrosse stick in sixth grade.) But I have been proud of the decisions she has made throughout her career and the way she has responded to the struggle of how to respond to coaching that challenges us instead of gives us a medal for participation.

The meaning we derive from sports is not all about us. I first learned this from my own father. I never questioned his coaching judgments. When he pulled me aside after my sophomore football season, he initiated the conversation. My dad played the best players for the good of the team and program, as varsity coaches should. He also encouraged me to work hard and stay positive. However, in addition, he also told me that he intentionally didn't play me enough quarters on special teams to earn my varsity letter. He felt it would mean more to me to earn it during my junior year, during which we won the state championship. He was right. Nepotism in youth sports isn't.

Coaching the way God would have us coach presents numerous difficulties. One of these is dealing with cuts. As a Xaverian Brothers sponsored school, my high school asked us to promote Xaverian values of compassion, humility, trust, zeal, and simplicity in all that we do. This is a tall order when someone is getting cut, and as coaches, we discuss this together on retreats. I have been called the most unchristian man in the world by one parent upset over her son's cut from basketball. I believe how we make cuts matters face-to-face, not by posting a list. This is the way of honesty with God in reconciliation. Face-to-face, we are forced to see the reality of our lives, our weaknesses and failings, but with hope for the future. Steve Langton was cut from freshman basketball. The *Salem Evening News* was doing a story on the difficulties of cuts for coaches. I pointed in the weight room and said, "See that guy? Ask him."

The interviewer brought him in the office and asked him what it was like to get cut from freshman basketball. Steve responded, "Devastating. Worst two weeks of my life. Thank God!"

"Thank God?" the interviewer asked. "Why 'Thank God'?"

Steve went on to recount how he was one of the best athletes from his town and felt humiliated when people would ask him about basketball and he had to say he got cut. He and others had high hopes for him. However, he couldn't throw the ball in the ocean. After being down for a few weeks, he decided to try winter track. Now he was a senior in high school, a state qualifier in three events, and going to college on an athletic scholarship. So *thank God!* God knew better what was in store for him. He just had to open up to the possibilities of life and the mystery of Coach God's involvement in it. Steve's story continued years later. Someone saw him working out at the gym and noticed his extraordinary athleticism. They asked him to come to the Olympic training center. Steve became a three-time Olympian and two-time bronze medalist bobsled pusher as a member of the American Olympic team. He later even competed on television's *Amazing Race*. Thank God Steve was humble enough to know that God had not only blessed him with athletic gifts, but also surrounded him with people who recognized them and helped him to become his best self!

Another difficulty a coach faces is deciding playing time. Equal time is not always equitable, but in youth sports, every growing child should have the opportunity to play. How else can they enjoy all that the sport has to offer? As a coach, I have been far from perfect in this regard. My most vivid failure involves the present University of Florida head football coach, Dan Mullen. I coached Dan in nine seasons between football, basketball, and track. However, it was in basketball I made my biggest mistake. I never started Dan until his last game of his senior year. He scored eighteen points. On the way out of the locker room, I said, "I'm sorry, Dan, I should have played you more." He smiled and replied, "That's okay, Coach. I forgive you."

I could not have been more humbled and was certainly not deserving of his compassion and mercy. Now I know that as a very high profile head coach, Coach Mullen works every day to try to make a difference in the lives of the young men entrusted to his care. All coaches need to be forgiven. We can't be paralyzed by the fear of making a mistake in our coaching decisions. But when we do, reconciliation sure can help our relationships if we are open to the Spirit of Coach God.

2

Believe in Excellence

This is much more than a tale of two quarterbacks. It is a tale about the pursuit of excellence, talented players, rivalry, and the greatest high school football game in the last century in Massachusetts' high school football. But most of all, it is the story of how Coach God wants us all to strive for excellence by using our talents and being the best people we can be. However, there is a nuance to the excellence Coach God demands of us. The best players play and everyone else becomes better people as a result. The challenge for coaches is determining at what level should the best people play? We are all competitive persons to some degree. Shouldn't winning be the only thing?

This story begins with Brian St. Pierre's decision to attend St. John's Prep. It probably was a foregone conclusion since his father had been a star at the school. He was now the team doctor, and Brian had grown up on the sidelines of school games. Brian was thrust into the starting quarterback role as a freshman on a very talented team. The tailback of that team was Rob Konrad, a six-foot-three, 235-lb. specimen with 4.45 speed who ended up playing nine years as the fullback for the Miami Dolphins (He had a pretty good career wearing number 44 at Syracuse too!). I used to stand seven yards in front of the center directing the scout defense. When Rob would burst up the middle and cut in front of me, I could feel the air move by me as he passed. He was legit. We also had a fullback, Brian Toner, of similar size and speed. So needless to say, we ran the ball—a lot.

We also asked the quarterback to not only throw the ball, but to run it on plays such as read veer. For those unfamiliar with football terminology, this play is where the quarterback places the ball in the abdominal region of the back then "reads" the defensive end. If he tackles the back, he pulls it out and runs around the end.

In the same freshman class were other talented athletes, including another quarterback, Brian Lentz. Brian Lentz was a powerful runner and a hard-nosed football player. But as a young player, he did not want to share the limelight. At the time, all varsity coaches besides the head coach and conditioning coach brought the varsity players who didn't play much to the sub-varsity game on Mondays. Our program believed that in all sub-varsity games, all players should play. Younger programs were for player development and provided parents an opportunity to see their sons perform in a sport they loved. It was only on the varsity level that we counted wins and losses, and even at that level, we tried to get seniors on the field. As a matter of fact, one year we played fifty-two seniors regularly in varsity games and still went undefeated in the regular season! At this particular sub-varsity game, we were playing at Catholic Memorial and alternating our quarterbacks during series, so another freshman quarterback was sharing the position. During the series Brian was out, he was not standing next to the offensive coordinator. He was not on the sideline rooting for his teammates. He was leaning against the field fence with helmet in hand, slouched. It looked like he was pouting. I approached him and asked him what he was doing. He explained that he thought he should be in the whole time. He did not like alternating series, and he hated losing. He felt that if he was in the whole game, it would benefit everyone. I explained that on the varsity level, the best people play, but on the sub-varsity level, everyone played. That was what was best for people. It encouraged sportsmanship, being a good teammate, and skill development. We didn't care about the outcome. We cared about effort and character. If he couldn't get off the fence and stand with his teammates, he would never play in our program. To his credit, he swallowed his pride, put on his helmet, joined his teammates, and began taking a journey that never would have happened for any of us on that championship team had he not responded with humility and maturity. After that season, he became a running back—a very powerful and hard-nosed running back. He even suffered a setback with a broken leg during his junior season. He became our feature back in the 1997 Game of the Century and a captain and real leader on that team.

As for Brian St. Pierre, he continued in his starting role for three years. He mentioned that in those years, I told him he was "too competitive." I suppose it must be true. Still, it was a little hard to believe since I am so competitive that no family members even want to play games with me, unless they are on my team. Actually, I don't know anyone who likes losing, especially to Xaverian. Which brings us to "the game."

We knew at the beginning of the 1997 season that we had a championship-caliber team. Several of our athletes were highly recruited, and all of the Boston sports media had us preseason number two, right behind number one Xaverian, our archrival. Now bear in mind, our head coach and their head coach are fast friends. We have even been on retreats together, and when their coach was sick, our head coach would bring soup up to his room. But there is no love lost on the field when these two programs collide. The papers had a weekly countdown until Thanksgiving Day when number one would meet number two. In the preseason, we decided that the only obstacles to reaching that goal was ourselves. Wayne Lucier, another captain who played several years with the New York Giants, approached our coaches and expressed that all they needed was for the coaches to remain positive. The coaches communicated that we needed the players to remain humble. So our head coach, Jim O'Leary, designed a T-shirt for us to wear with humility. On the front, it said, "TEAM." It was a constant reminder for each talented athlete to check his ego at the door. We also had a sign above the door that we tapped on the way out of our locker room to games, similar to Notre Dame's "Play Like a Champion Today" sign. We even carried a travel sign on our bus that we tapped as we exit the bus for away games. It didn't say, Believe in Mediocrity, Give a Decent Effort, or Think About Excellence. It stated, "*Believe* in Excellence."

In order to believe in excellence the best players have to play. It is only fair. There are talent differences in athletes. Coach God blessed us with different talents. If a coach recognizes talents, then everyone else can find their role. Since they are multitalented athletes, they too can achieve excellence, and we can achieve it together. That makes a true TEAM. More importantly, on the back of the T-shirts was a litany of reminders of what it would take to pursue excellence as a *team*. It read like this:

1. I will always put the team before any individual goal.
2. I will always support my teammates in a positive manner.
3. I will believe in and pursue excellence in every practice and game.
4. I will never display any disrespectful remarks or actions to officials or opponents.
5. I will work harder to make myself a better player and person every day.
6. I will believe in my teammates and help them make good choices.
7. I will play hard.
8. I will believe.
9. I will make any sacrifice to help my team succeed.
10. I will make my teammates proud of me.
11. Win or lose, this is my team, and I will make no excuses for my team or myself.
12. You are my team.
13. We will achieve as one.

We read this every weak as a team with a different player reading each line. Even then, we still needed constant reminders. Our quarterback, Brian St. Pierre, was injured in the opening game. His backup, Alan Rich, started in his place. We knew that we had to rally around our inexperienced quarterback. As we were heading out to warm-ups at our away game at Barnstable High School, one of our players yelled, "They are here to see *the show*."

Brian St. Pierre quickly and emphatically yelled, "I don't want to hear that! We aren't the show until we win the state title! Everyone has to do their job and take care of business!"

On the very first possession, our middle linebacker, Rob Robichaud, laid a hit on the sideline that could be heard throughout the stadium. It energized our players as a statement play that set the tone for the game. Rob hadn't even played in a varsity game until the previous week. He had been sharing time as expected in the sub-varsity games since freshman year. Remember those two six-foot-three, 245-lb. running backs. They were the varsity linebackers in Rob's freshman year. The best play. His senior year, Rob was the best, although he was only five-eight and 180 pounds. We won. We won every game as the countdown continued in the papers, and we won by similar scores against common opponents of Xaverian.

Finally came the day of "the game." It was Thanksgiving Day 1997. Thanksgiving football is special around the country but particularly in New England where century-old rivalry games are played between high schools. On Thanksgiving Day, families and teammates gather both the night before and on game day to renew old friendships and embellish old memories. When I arrived at six for a ten o'clock game, there were already fans in the stands in twenty-degree weather, staking out their seats. My own extended family came later and couldn't even get in. They watched from an adjoining hill overlooking the stadium. The game itself was a hard-hitting affair as expected with Xaverian leading until late in the third quarter, 14–7. Brian St. Pierre kept the ball on a read veer and sprinted thirty-five yards to pay dirt. Now Brian will probably argue with me about this. As our latest head coach, he enjoys arguing with me anyway. But he is a better passer than runner. After all, he was an award-winning quarterback at Boston College and played eight seasons as an NFL quarterback. Our marquee runner was the former freshman quarterback who made critical first downs and touchdowns multiple times on mental toughness and second and third effort that season. So while Xaverian pummeled our running back on the read fake, Brian St. Pierre scampered down the sideline and into the end zone. We decided to go for two and in an unusual way. We ran right behind our right guard, Wayne Campbell. This was risky as not only would Xaverian be keying our running back; but Wayne had only started this game due to our putting future NFL lineman Wayne Lucier in the backfield in a power I-formation. He was expected to block an All-Conference defensive tackle lined up opposite him, and this was a formidable challenge. Wayne drove him several yards back, our running back ran the ball right behind him into the end zone, and the rest of the fourth quarter slugged its way into Massachusetts' high school football history. One can read the details of the game in news reports of the time, but the real details lie in the T-shirt in TEAM, in *believing* in excellence, and in the best players playing. Once we executed this part of the game plan, everything else fell into place.

However, when Coach God tells us to be our very best, God means more than this. "Love your neighbor as I have loved you." He also expects us to love each other. Even our opponent when the rivalry game is over. I recently ran into Wayne Campbell while shopping with my daughter. I introduced him as the player that led us to victory in the 1997 championship game, and he said, "I love your father." I replied, "I love you too, Wayne."

My daughter didn't know what to make of it. She asked why. Coaches and players today don't even talk that way anymore. They are afraid to say it even though they may feel it. We are all aware of the boundaries that have been crossed by unscrupulous adults that should never have been in such positions of trust. As a result, young people don't hear "I love you" from their coaches, only from their family. And yet there are so many coaches who are the expression of God's love for the aspiring athlete. It is a shame neither of us knew how to respond, so we both shrugged and said, "Because we do." This is also part of the excellence we believe in, the habit of excellence of love. When a coach does their best to evaluate talent, play the best, and help others find their role, they encourage a community of love. It is virtuous. The wisdom is in discerning the right thing to do at the right time. For that, we need to be people of prayer and depend upon Coach God.

3

The Pursuit of Happiness and God's Will

Coaches coach, players play, and parents parent. Every year, a local sportswriter publishes a yearly reminder to young athletes and their parents about this mantra. Just like on a team whenever everyone fulfills their roles, the team achieves together. We all need to fulfill our role in the community in order for us to achieve happiness. Although Jesus said, "No father gives his son a stone when he asks for a fish," we all know that giving our sons and daughters everything they want is not the way to achieve happiness. Coach God certainly asked his son to do unpleasant things, like death on a cross! Jesus could have rejected his role in providing a way for us to attain eternal happiness, instead he prayed, "Father, let this cup pass me by, but if it is your will, I will do it." Was he putting his Father first, his Coach, humanity, or in being true to himself, was he serving all three?

Coaches coach. A coach cannot be constantly worried about playing time for each individual on a team while managing a game. Those individual interests, if catered to, can reinforce the selfish inertia of humans, which leads to the great unhappiness for even the beneficiary of exceptional treatment. Besides, if you add up all of the minutes spent by coaches and players practicing together in the game that they love, the amount of time playing the game they love far exceeds the playing time of a game. For professional coaches, they are paid to execute the mission of the organization. At the higher levels, if they are not successful (winning), they are fired or resign. They are doing a job, and even high school varsity sports can resemble a business. This gets even more complicated by the business of college scholarships, and high school coaches have lost much of the influence they used to have because of this focus on the future. Travel teams, showcases, and camps all promise not only skill development, but also a future bright with an education paid for by the business of sport. The players are with their marketers for the majority of their youth, not their coaches who only see them daily for three months of the year.

The recent field of study of positive psychology has something to say about this. Once we find our strengths, we achieve happiness by using our strengths for something greater than ourselves to achieve meaning. If we use our strengths for ourselves, we will miss the meaning. Moreover, we cannot savor the moments of the sport we love playing if we are mentally always in the future. How many times has one heard of players being "in a zone," lost in the ecstasy of the moment in their sport? While hope for the future is important, greed is not. Avarice strips us of our capacity for true happiness and even joy. We should appreciate our experiences as we are experiencing them instead of always seeing them as a means to an end. Similar to our greatest sports moments, we should savor God's presence by being fully present to occasions of God's grace. I have come to know that for most young people God is to be found in the present. When we engage in mindfulness or centering meditations, they become aware of God's presence in a way that they had not experienced before. By helping our young athletes live in the present and appreciate the time with us instead of being forever forward-looking, we prepare them for being still and encountering Coach God in the sacredness of the moment.

When I was a head varsity basketball coach in my mid-twenties, I was not happy. I took losses too personally, and I didn't like who it was making me. This was odd because I loved basketball. I still do. I used to dribble my ball to the town courts, play all day, and dribble it back home, stopping only at the church to say "hi" to God. I was fortunate enough to go on a retreat that asked some simple questions:

1. What area of your life is giving you difficulty?
2. What are your satisfactions with it?
3. What are your dissatisfactions with it?
4. What kind of person is it making you?
5. What meaning does it have in your life?
6. What meaning would you like it to have?
7. How do you get there?

After reflecting, journaling, and sharing my thoughts with another retreatant, I found that I at least had a pathway back to happiness. More importantly, it provided a simple formula for helping players achieve happiness.

Players play. Mark Collura also loved basketball until his junior year. In January of his junior year, Mark told me he was thinking of quitting varsity basketball. Now first off, I was raised with the idea of once a quitter always a quitter. If you start something, you see it through to the end. But I tried not to impose my view on Mark. I asked to see him after school to ascertain why he wanted to quit. It was, of course, about playing time but also deeper than that. He was only getting two minutes of time a game, which was frustrating, but he also felt as if he had lost his love for the game. One other element of positive psychology is remembering the past with fondness instead of regret or guilt. So we spent the afternoon as I had on retreat wrestling with those questions. I told Mark how my junior high coach, Don Gagner, had us all close our eyes and listen to a swish as the ball dropped through the net. I still love that sound! Mark began to remember all of the things he loved about basketball. He started going to practice and working on his midrange jumper. He enjoyed the flow of the game and quick transitions as a member of the scout team in late practice scrimmages. He smiled again. He achieved happiness by playing the sport he loved without worrying about the future. What happened after that? Mark was voted a captain by his teammates his senior year, averaged twenty points a game, and actually did attend college on a basketball scholarship. He may never have done this if he decided he wouldn't play.

Parents parent. On one occasion, a basketball player's parent was yelling out at his son on every possession, telling him what to do, and screaming at him whenever he made a mistake on the court. This led to his son playing very nervously, and his turnovers and missed shots multiplied. After the game, I asked him how he felt. He said he felt humiliated. I asked him if he minded if I spoke to his dad, and he gave me permission. Once we went up into the gym, I asked the father if I could speak to him a moment. I told him how his son was feeling. His father was crushed. Tearfully, he told me that all he wanted was for his son to succeed and be happy. We both agreed that I would take care of the critique of his play on and off the court, and he would manage the car ride home and the dinner table. Everyone was much happier. There is an axiom in coaching that you can't coach the dinner table. Nor should we. The dinner table should be a place to share one's day, one's highs and lows with the ones who love you most. A coach can never love a player as much as a parent loves their son or daughter. Their relationship is transitory. If one is lucky, there are a few player-coach relationships that last a lifetime.

When this player was a senior, we ended his first practice with a situation. Early in my career, I decided to end practices with a situation game like down two points with five seconds left on a full court inbound so that by the end of the season, we had played out sixty situations. This is because every good state tournament game comes down to how one plays the last two minutes. We went to a classroom. As the rest of the team listened, this player and I sim-ulated a car ride home when the player was upset over the coach, playing time, jealousy, the officials, or a loss. The situation could change to whatever would lead the player to scapegoating behavior and narcissism. The parent would start with a phrase that began with "I can't believe." The player had to respond in a way that allowed their parent to be a parent that deeply cared about them but did not allow them to become the coach or the teammate. He handled his role admirably, and I continued the role play for many years. I also found situations when someone would come off the bench and hit a game-winning three-pointer then leave practice exhilarated instead of exhausted, swarmed by his teammates in the absence of the crowd.

Then they could go home and share what happened at their supper table, and we all would be happy. Coach God also puts in situation games. God invites us to share our successes and failures around a table every week. Some of these situations are tough and end in tears of sorrow, not joy. They plunge us into purgative phases of our spiritual journey—our *Dark Night of the Soul*, if you will. Coach William Britton described one of these situations to me as we drove the equipment van up to football camp in Maine some summers ago. He told me, "In '93, at a time when my life was in free fall, I had a spiritual experience that led to a profound change in direction, a change that would never have occurred if not for the sound of my long dead father's voice. "Just find a way to be happy, Will."

I was on the road coming back from Dixville Notch at the end of what Eugene O'Neil once called "a long day's journey into night." Seven hours of driving punctuated by an overwhelming sense of loneliness, a tearful recognition that I was, like the lost combat veteran of Springsteen's reverie, "a rider on a downbound train."

"The eighties had been a decade of loss most profoundly defined by the death of my father in '85, the failure of a business I had given my all to save, and most severely by the accidental death of my twenty-year-old son John in a senseless industrial accident in the fall of '89. I turned fifty in '92, and these losses, among others, brought me hard upon the awful realization that I was careening down a road of self-destruction. For many years, I'd felt trapped in a career field that I loathed. When stripped to its essence, I sold commercial tires for a living. That was just a paycheck, a way to pay the bills. I hated it! There's just no other accurate way to say it. I'd never contemplated suicide but saw myself a failure with little to live for and almost nothing in the way of self-esteem. By the early nineties, it is not too much to say I would have welcomed death. Approaching Franconia Notch from the north that night with tears streaming down my face in a dreamlike state, I turned to my right to see the profile of the Old Man in the Mountain, the Great Stone Face as Hawthorne had christened this visage. The stars were bright. For a moment, there appeared a chain of moons that seemed to emanate directly from the old man's eyes. This bracelet made of silvery disks passed before me in the sky, and in each disk appeared a face—the members of my family who'd passed away in the course of my lifetime. Some of these folks I'd barely known but there they were in order of their passing. Each engaged my eyes in what seemed to me the most benign of smiles as they moved across my line of sight in slow procession, blinking out as they moved toward the far side of the Notch. Then in very close procession came my father and my son. But this made sense, I'd thought of them often and always together in some spiritual dimension. In fact, I'd written this poem about the place 'across the River Styx' of my imagination:

Elysium

In mythic fields,
my father and my son,
the glow of autumn burning in their eyes,
toss a football,
share a knowing smile.
And wait for me.

"While John's face passed before me without direct remark, the moon that carried my father's face expanded to the fullness of the Notch and carried what I felt was my father's spirit to and through my body. In unmistakable tones, I heard my father's voice. His message was simple and direct. "Just find a way to be happy, Will." His presence lingered for a bit and then was gone. The twilight of the Notch regained its place, but not before a large white bird flew right at me then veered to hit the rearview mirror on the driver's side of the pickup truck I was driving. I looked immediately into the mirror to see the body of the bird, but there was nothing there to see. He called me Will, something no one else in the realm of my memory had ever done. He called me Will with regularity throughout our lives together."

Within a week of this vision, Bill's cousin, Marcia, came to him with a catalog describing a program of study at Salem State College leading to a master's degree in English with a writing concentration. She knew the state Bill was in and said, "You need a change of direction. You need to find meaning and purpose again in your life. Maybe this is a path you should follow."

Bill took the catalog, and embarked on a remarkable journey that led to him completing his Master's degree in 1998 and beginning a teaching and coaching career at St. John's Prep. He has blessed our team over the years with his reflections on what it means to be a warrior. In this talk Bill emphasizes that true leaders care for the most vulnerable in the community; they are not about themselves, but rather for others. But what has always stuck in my mind is his vision of his father and his father's urging him to pursue happiness. For Bill, he wonders sometimes if it was a "hallucination", for as secular humanist he does not explicitly confess a relationship with Coach God. Still, he states, "The experience has taken me on the journey of my lifetime and has brought meaning and purpose to my life I never thought to know. But, now and then my dreams take me back to Franconia Notch in the darkness of 93' and I hear my father's voice at the core of my being. "Just find a way to be happy, Will."

For me, I recognize the familiar pattern of God's game plan in our spiritual lives in Bill's story. Together with Coach God, our happiness is sometimes only realized through the crucible of suffering and loss. Moreover, God does not only communicate with us at the ten o' clock mass on Sundays, through reflection on readings, or our speculative intellect assenting to theological truths. God also reveals to us through our imagination! God is essentially communicative and seeks us more than we seek God. God will use whatever means necessary to assure us of God's loving presence, including dreams and visions. These are moments of grace if we are open to our dependence upon God and are followed by God's ability to bring us insight through various means of communicating God's Word. These moments of grace can create new life and meaning in our lives. Ultimately, we become closer to our Coach God, ourselves, and our loved ones through the cycle of this spiritual journey, even in death. I cannot tell my friend Bill the meaning of his experience with his father nor can I tell anyone the meaning of one's suffering and loss. Bill and I agree on this mystery as he shared with me this poem:

The Visit

The old man's eyes
Project a ray of light
A chain of moons
Across the line of sight
And in each disk a face.
While in the Notch below,
My living presence looms
And is transfixed in somber recognition
Of the family dead.
From first to last across the generations
I have known.

Ambience of light,
A trick of sad imagination
In the tumult of a failing life.
I'll never know
And yet…

And yet, if we are willing to pursue happiness by entering into this mystery, by ceasing to control what is beyond our grasp and trusting enough to "let go and let God," God will guide us and make God's loving presence known to us. These assurances of God's love can be the most meaningful moments of our athletic spiritual life!

4

In the Hands of an Angry God

Conditioning is essential for any athlete. Sometimes the words used for conditioning, which involves running, indicate something more painful or difficult. Think about the most common basketball conditioning drill. It starts on the end line, sprinting to touch the foul line then back, half court then back, three-quarter court then back, and full court and back. This drill is commonly called a suicide. They are usually run to condition an athlete to perform when physically fatigued, especially in fourth-quarter pressure situations. A player will take a pressure-packed foul shot. The team will run or not run contingent on the outcome of the foul shot. It helps a coach train and evaluate mental toughness or who can keep their shooting form consistent amidst distractions and fatigue. That is why they are called free throws. The player is in control of the outcome, depending on their mental toughness and repetition of good form and work habits during off-season individual time. Good shooters don't develop in ten foul shots at the end of practice. They develop when a person is by themselves with their basketball, working on their game. Other conditioning drills involve hill running or "gassers," which push the limits until the player is feeling out of gas with nothing left in the tank. Players are expected to report in shape. If they have not had the self-discipline to do this, the coach is expected to get them in shape. Teammates are expected to encourage the struggling players, sometimes even doing more than verbally supporting them. I have seen players literally help carry players across the finish line. It promotes an attitude of teamwork, sometimes even in opposition to the coach who is causing such agony.

However, during my coaching career, I have seen quite a shift in perceptions of this conditioning. Some parents and coaches now see this running as a punishment, and the original intent is threatened to be lost. I first encountered this upon coming to St. John's Prep. I had been a head track-and-field coach and a head basketball coach in New Hampshire. I had never seen a problem with end-of-practice conditioning. As a matter of fact, a state champion sprinter I coached used to go do more workout sprints after practice, which led to a big breakthrough for him. Pat Connaughton of the Portland Trailblazers and Baltimore Orioles, whom I coached all four years of high school basketball, used to do his own workouts with a weighted vest in addition to our grueling workouts. That is why when he had such amazing numbers at the NBA combine neither he nor I was surprised. The legendary track coach at St. John's, Ray Carey asked why in basketball I was taking a sport, running, and making it into something that felt like a punishment. This seemed inherently contradictory to him as he and I both tried to find athletes in the school who loved running, especially if they were fast and loved to do repetitions of sprints to get even faster. He changed my way of thinking as a basketball coach. I decided to run transition drills, fast break drills or quick change-of-possession drills before putting someone on the foul line to test their skill and mental toughness. This more closely simulated real game experience. After all, when do basketball players bend down to touch a line on the floor during games? These drills, along with the previously mentioned situation games, seemed more appropriate for everyone to leave practice better prepared, in condition, and feeling positive.

This led to many philosophical discussions about conditioning in my rental apartment. I was living with Steve Clifford, an assistant coach at Boston University. Steve coached many years as an assistant coach in the NBA before becoming the head coach of the Charlotte Hornets He used to ask me, "What do you do with the selfish player, the player who doesn't want to practice hard that day? They want you to sit them out because they don't want to work hard. But if you keep them in, everyone suffers." I did not have an answer. I knew that if the whole team was made to run, it would somewhat fit the situation because when one of us doesn't do our job, the whole community or team suffers. Still, I knew that it was patently unfair to the players who were working as hard as possible. It wasn't like when teachers threaten to give the whole class detention if the perpetrator of some prank doesn't come forward. There was no need to pressure a community to get an individual to take responsibility. Everyone knows who the irresponsible person is, and the player's lack of integrity and self-discipline necessitates a disciplinarian. But how can this disciplinarian aid the spiritual growth of the player without being seen as a corporal punisher, even a potentially criminal one? The answer lies in the letter to the Hebrews. It speaks of how like a Father, God chastises those he loves. He reproves them and subjects them to discipline for a time, not as punishment, but to impede the selfish inertia of the individual that is harmful to them and everyone around them.

I was lucky enough to assist a tremendous basketball coach named Sean Connolly. He was once the all-time leading scorer in Massachusetts high school history, even scoring over forty points in a game I coached against him while battling bacterial meningitis! He went on to a successful career at Ohio State. When he took over the program on the varsity level, he instituted a running consequence for every competitive situation, full court one-on-one drills, foul shooting, and scrimmaging. Everything had a winner and a loser. Athletes were always under pressure to perform to the best of their ability. He changed my mind about running as a basketball coach. I saw players respond calmly to pressure situations with a reservoir of physical and mental toughness that they didn't previously hold. Selfishness wasn't allowed. Everyone was expected to try their very best; if they didn't, there was a consequence. Isn't that the way it is in life? Think of all of the situations when people expect us to show up and make our best effort. Are there not far-reaching consequences if they don't? In molding these young men in the way he did, I feel Sean Connolly was acting as Coach God was in the letter to Hebrews. The scripture says he is acting like a Father, but since Sean was so young at the time,

I think few of the players saw him as a father figure. Nevertheless, he had the wisdom to treat them with the same type of tough love that God treats us. I have worked under some very talented head coaches. Former NFL quarterback Brian St. Pierre is one of those coaches. This year, we started the seasons 1–2. In a team meeting, Brian called out the team and told them the root of the problem as he saw it was they were entitled and selfish. I was so happy to hear him say that!

So many coaches shy away from those assessments because they don't want to deal with any negative feedback from parents and then administrators. It wasn't a secret. There was empirical evidence of laziness. People have become afraid to name things as they are. Sin has fallen out of our vocabulary. But what else could you call extreme self-centeredness, finger-pointing and blaming anyone but oneself? The officials, the coach, the fellow players, and the lazy or selfish players will all fail to take responsibility unless the courageous or self-assured coach names the infraction specifically and provides the remedy. That remedy might be conditioning, so we started conditioning more. You can guess what happened. Our season turned around. On bus rides from away games, players got their faces out of their phones, sang and rejoiced over victories, and overtly expressed thanks to God that Coach St. Pierre had made them run. They dominated fourth quarters when other teams fatigued. NBA coach, Steve Clifford had it right. We can overcome the selfishness and lack of self-discipline with team discipline—like going off on the right snap count—or there is a consequence.

The best coaches I know believe in overloading the best players and their best teams. Sometimes they might practice basketball drills three on five in order to learn to handle pressure. Sometimes they put a younger player in a pressure situation so they learn how to handle challenges with courage and resiliency. It is a challenge for that coach to have the wisdom to gauge how much pressure one can put on to draw out that player's best. When we face life's hardships, it is understandable that we question God like Job or rail against God as if he is that mean coach who made us run or made practice so hard. That coach loves you. As Aristotle said, "Practice doesn't make perfect." No one plays a perfect game. Practice makes permanent. Difficult practices lead to easier experiences when results count in games and in life! If we need to work on some habits of excellence in our life, such as humility or courage, it may seem that God is angry with us, but God is just coaching us up to be our best selves! Eventually we will also realize that and be able to thank Coach God!

5

God Loves a Loser

"If we lose this playoff game, I don't want to see any of you boys crying. Men don't cry!" I heard these words once as an assistant coach for a middle school aged boys' basketball team. Now I have always prided myself on being a loyal assistant coach. Just like the principal, the head coach is the only person who talks to everyone, all constituents. So I figure my job is to assist, suggest, and support, not to decide policy or contradict. I have never publicly contradicted a head coach in front of the team. I intentionally decided not to assist multiple coaches throughout my career if their philosophy or teaching to young people differed from mine or Coach God's. However, this was the first time I felt I had to step forward. I explained to the boys that the coach and I disagreed. The previous week, I was in the locker room at Boston Garden. We just lost the North Finals in the last two minutes, and players were devastated. It wasn't the last game for most of them as we were an underclass team, but there was a lot of crying going on.

There is too little crying these days. With our faces in our screens too often, we know a little about a lot but are slowly losing the depth that comes with allowing ourselves to empathize, to feel compassion, and to contemplate the meaning of suffering in our lives. Feeling something while playing sports, even during loss, is a gift from Coach God. It means we have passion for our sport. We care about our teammates. We care about winning, but we also embrace losing as we embrace each other. They may not learn that if their whole experience in sport is marked by the "everyone gets a medal" mentality. Coach God gave us tear ducts for a reason. I shared with them the story of a senior football player who was photographed on the field crying after one of our state championship losses. He was ridiculed in school and in the media. He heard from people from other states criticizing him. He felt humiliated. We have stayed in touch. He has never cried since. Even when his wife's mother died, he was unable to cry with her. The tears wouldn't flow even though he longed for them to come out. I wanted better for them. I wanted them to be fully human, just like Coach God wanted for his son. The shortest line in the scriptures is "And Jesus wept." A short line but very powerful. Coach God wanted his son to enter fully into the human condition. He wept at the loss of his friend, Lazarus. So they should cry. In losing, all feelings should be validated by the coach, just like in life Coach God listens to us and trusts that we will be okay. We can't prevent the loss. Sixty-three out of sixty-four teams end with locker rooms like ours in the NCAA basketball tournament. But we can support people through the tough times as Coach God supports us! Luckily, my friend, the head coach now agreed. When we lost our final game the following year, our friendship, the families we met, and the friendships my son made have endured, they had depth.

When I was helping coach my daughter's eighth grade team in my spare time, we had an improbable run that put us into the championship game. Once again, a middle school coach told the athletes at our last practice (girls this time) that he didn't want to see any tears after the game. This time I not only repeated my story of the Boston Garden, but on the way to the game, I rode with the head coach. I told him that this was the last time I would ever get to coach my daughter since my high school is all-boys. My daughter and I had gone to the gym every Sunday for four years to shoot hoops, both for skill development and for our mutual love of basketball. I told him not to be afraid to be emotional as this was not only his last game to coach his daughter, but also his children or any player he coached. He took us into the auditorium at the school we were visiting and gave a very emotional pregame speech to the girls. We won. After the game, there were tears of joy and lots of embracing! I put my arm around him and said, "See, it wasn't so bad to get emotional, was it?"

The worst loss I have ever experienced also spoke the most to me about Coach God's presence to support us and the mystery of how things work out in sports. We were 12–0 in 2001, and our team was laden with college prospects and future professional athletes. Our quarterback was John McCarthy (professional hockey and Olympian), receiver Matt Antonelli (professional baseball), and running back Jonathan Goff (professional football). The other athletes were going on to play at places like University of Notre Dame, Colgate University, and Boston College. In a hard-hitting state championship against our nemesis, Everett High School, the game came down to the fourth quarter. We outgained them 2–1 in yardage, sent several key players to their sideline with injuries, and, except for two plays, dominated the game. Still we found ourselves behind as time was winding down. We executed a long drive to have a chance to win in the last minute. Our former tailback, Steve Van Note, was now a fullback. He worked back from a season-ending knee injury during his junior year to have a stellar season. John handed the ball off to him. As he approached the three-yard line, an Everett player put his helmet on the ball and it came loose. As it tumbled toward the end zone, it felt like a scene from a Rocky movie where Burgess Meredith is yelling "Nooo!" in silent slow motion as Rocky is falling to the mat. Everything slowed down as the ball kept bouncing and bouncing. Then things sped up, and there was a mad scramble for the ball with multiple players from each team diving for it and kicking it. It moved toward the back of the end zone where an Everett player fell on it. Game over! We were all devastated, but Steven was inconsolable. Several players tried to talk to him, but he didn't respond. He just tearfully made his way to the bus.

I didn't talk to him until after everyone had showered. Steven and I knew each other pretty well since he had been a camp counselor for me for several years. I told him I was sorry for what happened and asked if he wanted to go out to eat. He said yes, and we went out for Chinese food for a few hours. As we talked over crab rangoon and fried rice, we both expressed that we couldn't believe what had happened. Both of us were taught there was no excuse for fumbling so he felt he had let down his team—a team that thought it was going to be the best team in Prep history, 13–0. Then we entered more deeply into the mystery of winning and losing and how Coach God deals with us. Steve had already proven to be a resilient athlete, having come back from a devastating injury. Had he not fumbled, it is entirely possible that the task of winning the game would have fallen on a much more fragile player, our placekicker. I don't know how that kicker would have handled making or missing a potential game-winning field goal, but in either scenario, I don't think he would have handled it as well as Steven fumbling or scoring. The ball was in his hands because it was meant to be in his hands. What he did with the reality of the ball leaving his hands was between him and Coach God, but I did not think it was meaningless. One often hears that things happen for a reason. Although I didn't know what the reason was, I'm sure that there was one. I was also sure that there was no better person to make a mistake in that situation than him. We talked about the cliché but true statement that lots of plays led to that one play.

John McCarthy threw a 99-yard pass interception. Their tight end caught a pass right in front of our safety. No one plays a perfect game, but these true clichés are small consolation for the athlete who missed the foul shot, struck out, or fumbled away any hope for a last-second win. Instead, we focused on his figurative broad shoulders, his love for his teammates, and his resiliency and entered into the mystery of what this meant in his life. Once we got back at school late that night, we embraced, and he said something I will never forget. "Thanks, Coach. I don't know what you saved me from, but you saved me from something."

In that moment, I was glad I could be there for him in a way that maybe a parent or teammate could not. The last fifteen years have made it more difficult for us to coach. Our society is filled with anxiety and fear for the safety and security of our children. I can't imagine any organization would encourage or allow a coach to go out to dinner on a Saturday night with a young player. Professional boundaries prevail against such interactions. This is a tremendous loss that threatens to harm our athletes more than the initial loss of the contest. How can we open them up to the mysterious presence of Coach God in each loss that they experience? And there will be many. God loves the loser. We must find ways to have supportive conversations with our athletes that prevent them from not only losing the game but also losing Coach God in the process.

6

I Had a Dream

I have been a part of multiple state championships. I experienced an undefeated "dream season" as a high school football player in 1976 and as a varsity basketball coach in 1985 in New Hampshire. Since moving to Massachusetts in 1990, I have also been an assistant coach on state championship football teams in 1997 and 2012 and as an assistant coach on our school's only state basketball championship in over a hundred years in 2011. I have also had the exciting opportunity to coach a high school game at Gillette Stadium, Fenway Park, and Boston Garden. These venues were often the places where miracles occurred or dreams came true for my favorite teams as both a youth and adult, and to coach there has been a thrill. However, none of these *dream seasons* compare to the very real dream football season of 2004.

I have been known to predict snow days in my classes, but I make it clear to my students that I am by no means a meteorological prophet. I wouldn't even whip up a sincere snowy day prayer out of selfish interests due to the harm weather events could cause others. However, knowing my penchant for predictions, the other coaches asked me for a prediction during our 2004 preseason. The previous year, I gave out religiously oriented stickers for players to put inside their helmets. On these stickers, they could dedicate their individual game or season to a loved one or even pray that Coach God will help them do their best that day. I had some leftover stickers so I took one and I wrote, "Chris Zardas will break his leg against a team in red." I stuck it upside down in Coach Dave McHenry's locker and never told anyone what it said during the season. I said we would look at it after the season. This may sound like a strange prediction for a coach to write, but I had a dream two years prior. In the dream, Chris Zardas, our star running back, was hit by multiple players in red and broke his leg. Chris came to football camp as a freshman. After one run from scrimmage, I sent him to the head coach after telling Chris he is a varsity running back and would no longer be with the underclassmen. Since I know that God reveals in dreams in both the Hebrew and Christian scriptures, I took this dream seriously and began praying for Chris during his sophomore year. I never told Chris or anyone else about the dream, especially because I did not want him to be nervous. Chris had terrorized opposing defenses for years, and I hoped it would continue. Still, I prayed for his health.

We started out that year 4–0 as the top-ranked team in the state. We travelled to Marshfield but we hit so much traffic that we arrived late. In order to do a quick warm-up, our coach chose a *pit drill*, which we hadn't done in pregame since the early 1990s in the corner of the end zone right before game time. Bill Gaffney rolled on the knee of Chris Zardas, and he went down with a knee injury. Our team was so deflated that we didn't even compete with Marshfield and lost 40–0. I thought, *That's strange. Chris hurt his leg but it wasn't in the manner I had envisioned.* We proceeded to lose the next few games until Chris returned. He worked hard in therapy to make his way back in time for our conference games. His return was against the last team we would play in red, Catholic Memorial, until we played Everett High School in the playoffs. During the course of the game, Chris ran a wide play to the right and was hit on our sideline from different directions by three opposing players. I was on the headsets on the sideline, and right in front of me, the substance of my dream from two years ago transpired! Chris was in pain and was helped off the sideline and over to the team orthopedist with tears rolling down his cheeks. I never saw him leave to go to the hospital, but I was convinced his leg was broken.

On Mondays, the varsity coaches took underclass players to their sub-varsity game so I wasn't around school that afternoon for conditioning. When I came to practice on Tuesday, I found Chris standing next to me in full pads. I asked him, "What are you doing here? I thought you were hurt."

He replied, "The doctor said my leg has never been better."

I told him, "That's great! I've been praying for you really hard. I'm really glad you are healthy."

We went on to win the rest of our games. When Chris scored on a two-point conversion, Prep beat Xaverian on their home field for the first time ever on Thanksgiving Day. I'm sure his parents, teammates, and other coaches were praying for Chris to be healthy as our success as a team clearly depended on his strong legs. You would think that this was the meaning of my most memorable dream season. But there is more to the story. After the season, we had a particularly bad windstorm on campus. I was in the faculty dining room when I saw Chris approach the register through the dining room window. I poked my head out the door and said, "Chris, once you pay, come on in here. I have a story for you."

When he came in, it took about 15 seconds to say that I had been praying for him for two years because of the dream I had two years prior. I said he may not want to tell others because they might think he is crazy, I am crazy, or both. He thanked me and left to walk across campus with his friends, Phil Rich and Ian Merry. I returned to my lunch uninterrupted until all three young men came running into the faculty dining room two minutes later. While crossing campus the three young men had just crossed the street from our cafeteria and were walking toward the back of our chapel. The windstorm toppled a huge pine tree and it came crashing down thirty feet in front of them. They came running back into the cafeteria and screamed, "Coach, we almost got killed by a huge tree that crashed down right in front of us! If you hadn't stopped Chris to tell him that story, we would have been killed! You saved our lives!"

I replied, "Maybe that is why I had that dream two years ago. Who knows?" I really believe that Coach God works in mysterious ways. I do not believe that my prayers healed Chris' leg even though

I do believe in the power of prayer. Other people were praying for Chris to heal.

After his final game, the Xaverian coach said to me, "Thank God he's graduating." I'll bet many Xaverian fans were praying he didn't return from his injury.

I believe more in the prayer we say before our games that humbly prays, "Your will be done." Coach God made revelations to many believers over the centuries through dreams and the power of our imaginations. I encourage athletes to dream and imagine the impossible. As Mary said, "nothing is impossible for God." We cannot control winning and losing or how the ball bounces. I also don't believe God cares so much about sports that God tries to control outcomes. The power of Coach God in our lives is having the faith to enter into the mystery of the relationship with God as we live life fully, including sports. Let's not forget my most memorable season was marked by a prediction that did not come true. My dream happened but Chris did not break his leg. Instead, the falling tree did not kill Chris, Ian, and Phil. Coach God was involved somehow, I just don't know how. I wasn't privy to the game plan, I was just part of it. So are you.

7

The Hail Mary Pass

T he Hail Mary pass, a last-ditch effort to win a game or a play of desperation. Or is it? I have witnessed many Hail Mary passes in my career. The most famous, of course, was Doug Flutie's pass to Gerard Phelan to beat Miami in 1984. That was not my most memorable Hail Mary pass. One Thanksgiving Day, Dan Ross, son of the former NFL tight end Dan Ross, connected with Lonnie Hill on a 65-yard bomb that Lonnie caught amidst three Xaverian defenders and fell into the end zone at the pylon to beat Xaverian with no time left on the clock. The sideline was so thick with fans one couldn't even see the result of the play, only the official's hands flying up to signal touchdown. The stands erupted and actually partially collapsed under the weight of the student section. Coaches, fans, parents, and players all sprinted to the end zone and were caught up in a delirious mélange of embraces and pig piles and exhaustion in tangled celebrations. Three hours later, I took my pulse as I arrived in Cape Cod for Thanksgiving dinner at the LaPointe household. My heart rate was 135. I was still living in that present moment truly thankful and excited.

That was also not my most memorable Hail Mary pass. The Hail Mary pass is not a play of desperation. It is a play of confidence and believing victory is still possible. It is practiced every year as teams prepare for those last-second opportunities in a game. Every team runs a two-minute drill, usually scripted by a coach in preparation for that week's contest. My most memorable Hail Mary pass was thrown by Coach God with full confidence that it would be caught. The victory would be won by another player there that day, Peter Frates.

In March of 2012, Peter Frates shared his diagnosis of amyotrophic lateral sclerosis (ALS) with his family. On that night, he looked directly at his mother and told her, "This is not going to happen for me, but it will provide opportunity for the people who come after me, the people who follow." Think about that. Think about Jesus. Pete was chosen specifically by Coach God on this earth to save people from this dreadful disease. He and his mother have absolute clarity on this. His career as a three-sport athlete at St. John's Prep and as a scholarship baseball player at Boston College prepared him for this mission in life. This disease was an opportunity coming to the Frates family and the world as grace, just as God's loving presence shared with us. Everything his mom and Pete had done in his life prepared him for this moment. Pete became Coach God's quarterback, receiver, and assistant coach all rolled into one. With courage, leadership, and grace, he gathered his team. His family, sports family, and former teammates came and stood with him. Together they completed and are still completing my most memorable Hail Mary pass. You may recognize the route that was run by the whole team in that worldwide phenomenon, the Ice Bucket Challenge!

As a youngster, Pete oozed spirit. As an infant, he got a staph infection and spent ten days in the hospital fighting that disease. Luckily for the world, Coach God was already preparing him for his servant-leadership role by giving him the heart of a champion. Like Mary, his mother Nancy has held all of her memories in her heart and has absolute spiritual clarity concerning what Coach God was doing with Pete from the time Coach God was forming him in the womb. Many of her friends asked for playdates with Pete because they wanted their sons and daughters to hang out with such a nice boy. I too wanted my son to hang out with Pete. I chose Pete as a counselor at Camp Christopher and primarily had him work with the eleven- and twelve-year-olds. As a young man with charisma and impeccable integrity, I wanted my son to model himself after Pete.

So I assigned Pete to his group in the hope that my son and the other dozen or so campers would have the opportunity to learn from him.

Opportunity is an important theme when one examines the Hail Mary pass. We used to have a quote in our locker room that said, "Luck is when preparation meets opportunity." The world is lucky to have Peter Frates. As his mother stated, "Sports made Pete the person he is to change the world." Every season, every practice was preparing him for this moment of grace. His development of mental toughness, discipline, and hope put him in a position to be God's prophet, being afflicted by terrible suffering to deliver God's timeless message, "Don't be afraid. I am with you." God is present to all of us. Peter Frates was chosen to remind us of God's presence, to show us the face of the disease in all of its horror, and to exhort us that we can do better and we can win!

When Pete started the Ice Bucket Challenge, it became an international and social media sensation. It spread the globe like wildfire, inspiring people's hearts with love and a desire to help. Hundreds of millions of dollars have been raised, and new drugs in development are now nearing release. Pete said that fateful night that he knew that this was not for him, but the people who would follow. His servant leadership, his courage, and his sense of purpose was so strong that he also wanted the media to show the world his suffering and put a face on ALS. Like the prophets of old, Pete has taken up what God has given him to offer hope to those who suffer from ALS and their families and friends. Pete has been very intentional in sharing his suffering with the world, and that suffering is ineffable. Last week, he had sepsis and almost died. Cardinal Sean O'Malley came and anointed him. Pete needs a straight catheterization every three hours. Most people consider themselves very unlucky if they have to endure this pain once in their life. Think about it, every three hours!

I remember seeing film of Lou Gehrig, the original famous person with ALS, which is now known as Lou Gehrig's disease. I never saw him in a wheelchair struggling to breathe or unable to speak without the aid of technology. Pete wants people to see his suffering and know what an ALS diagnosis really means for the person and their families who will live with this disease. The Romans put Jesus very publicly on a cross to intimidate and cause fear. Pete successfully used the media to publicly display his cross to inspire compassion and hope. In sports, some leaders, both coaches and athletes, think being a leader is about power and threats. Look at the gift of Pete's cross as we look upon the cross of Jesus. It is the central symbol of our faith. What was thought to be folly and a failure has become a powerful symbol of hope through the self-sacrifice of one man being true to who Coach God called him to be.

As Nancy Frates told me, "You can lead through intimidation and a lot of talk, but Pete has led by kindness and by example." He is the ultimate team player and servant-leader, a modern-day suffering servant leading us to the freedom that comes with trusting in the game plan. Wherever Nancy Frates travels across the globe, strangers come up to her and thank her and Pete. Nancy herself has become more like Pete in the process. Her original vision was to save Pete. Why wouldn't it be? Do we think Mary really wanted to see her son Jesus suffer on the cross? Now Nancy also works tirelessly for those who will follow. If she could, she would go back to the days of no disease in a heartbeat, but she does not have any anger at Coach God for putting her and Pete in the game for this Hail Mary pass. She embraces it as a moment of grace. Some family members have been angry, not seeing Pete's suffering as grace. This is a normal reaction, even healthy. I remember being unable to pray for a whole year except to utter, "Lord, have mercy" when my niece Clare was dying of leukemia at two years old. Nancy has had some help in embracing her response to Coach God's call to get off the sidelines and into the game. She had external confirmation that God is with them. She had the support of many courageous women, including her mother-in-law who, although deceased, still talks to Pete. She has been blessed with an amazing daughter-in-law Julie and a granddaughter Lucy who brings joy into all of their lives. She has been supported by the mother of Jesus and her spiritual mother, Mary. She has found consolation at the Carmelite chapel as well as hope and peace in meditating on the pink flower in the beautiful stained glass there. When talking with Nancy, I reminded her that Pete's mission was contingent upon her yes, her "fiat" to what Coach God was asking of her son. When Juan Diego was given flowers by Mary to deliver her message to the bishop of Mexico City, she reminded him, "Am I not here, I, who am your mother?" This abiding presence of Mary's intercessory love has sustained Nancy as she, like Mary, has courageously supported her son in the same ways that she supported Jesus, let go, and let Coach God work with his player to complete the most amazing Hail Mary pass! A Hail Mary pass ends a game and sometimes a season. This Hail Mary pass continues.

Peter said as he shared his diagnosis, "I'm doing this for those who will follow." The challenge continues. How should one proceed? What is the game plan? When Nancy attended mass one week after the diagnosis, the priest gave a sermon about a farmer asking his son to go check on the well-being of animals. The son stood in the doorway, looking out at the deep, foreboding blackness. "I'm afraid. How will I see how to get there?" he asked. The father gave him a lantern and said, "Hold this light up then you can see how far to go safely. Then you put it down and walk. When you reach where you know it is safe, hold the light up again and then proceed one circle of light at a time." Coach God is our Father. He knows we are afraid. ALS is terrifying, but he has given us a light, Peter Frates, to hold up to guide our way. God is to be found in the present. Each moment is a moment of grace if we live in it. Pete's moments are filled with suffering but they are still occasions of grace for him, for us, and as light for the world! He continually reminds us to believe and don't give up hope! You can do it! I have prepared you! Now go win with the Hail Mary pass!

8

St. Pat's Day

When one witnesses a true leader, one recognizes it. Many student athletes consider themselves "leaders." They write it on their college resumes, but it may as well say bully, prima donna, or popular-vote winner. Anyone who watched the only state championship in St. John's Prep's history witnessed a true leader, a servant-leader.

My first memory of Pat Connaughton was in his first basketball game as a freshman in a junior varsity game at Boston English. In the first half, he scored sixteen straight points, including a step back three and a dunk in traffic. I left the stands, walked toward the junior varsity coach, tapped him on the shoulder, and said, "You won't be seeing him anymore!" Pat had eight points in the second half of the varsity game that night. He went on to be the highest scorer in St. John's Prep's history and led our team to its only basketball state title in over a hundred years.

Pat is a tremendous athlete. When I was growing up, I knew very few multiple-sport professional athletes: Danny Ainge, Michael Jordan, and Bo Jackson. They all were professional baseball players like Pat, and two of the three were also basketball players. Pat was initially signed by the Baltimore Orioles but he is currently playing for the Portland Trailblazers in the NBA. Looking back, it really didn't seem like I was in the presence of such greatness, but I was. His greatness wasn't in his athleticism, like the aforementioned players I idolized; it was in his humility. His teammates followed him because he was interested in making them all better. He played point guard when we needed a point guard, forward when we needed a forward, and did anything the coaches asked from him. No one else on the team ever questioned a coaching decision because Pat was loyal and did what was asked. I was responsible for pulling Pat out of the game if he wasn't playing great team defense. Sometimes he would just direct traffic under the hoop instead of truly defending screens, bumping cutters, and switching men. Pat and I also worked hard at taking charges. I would playfully jump out at him from behind trees, doors, or anything I could step out from on campus to get him to plant his feet, hold his spot, and take a charge. He got so good at it he even helped Notre Dame beat Detroit in his first collegiate game by taking a game-changing charge. Many selfish players won't take charges in high school, saving their body from the punishment it would take. Pat was self-sacrificing in every aspect of the game.

Some of the best evidence of his lack of ego is in his relationship with the Fidelity House in Arlington. He was especially grateful for the late Tim Graham. "Mr. Graham was always good to me and tough on me when he needed to be, but he was always fair. He often let me stay when I was in first and second grade and play the next hour with the third and fourth graders. But during the first hour, he wouldn't let me shoot until the game was on the line, stressing leadership and the importance of making your teammates better. He would pull you aside and be stern if needed and would always expect more out of you if he thought you could do it. He made sure I carried myself in a way a professional would, even as a nine-year-old. Showboating was never allowed or else you would be held out of games the following week!" From fifth to eighth grade, Pat always went back to referee the younger games for Coach Graham as a way to express thanks for the lessons he learned at Fidelity House. He always made time for the young athletes when he was at home. He never forgot his roots. Anyone who has ever seen Pat play when Portland is at the Garden could see his love for the hundreds of children from Fidelity House filling the stands to cheer him on. They would all wait around to see Pat after the game as he came up into the stands and waded through the sea of children, greeting each one personally until he has to leave with the team.

As a professional athlete, Pat used his success to lift up everyone else, especially disadvantaged children, children with cancer, and adults in need of financial assistance for higher education. We used to talk about his focal point on his shot. Now he speaks passionately about the focal point of his philanthropy. When I asked him why he started With Us Foundation, he told me, "Something I have noticed as I've gone from level to level is the fan following that athletes receive. But one thing I have always prided myself on is staying true to the person I've always been and to the people and places that have helped me get to where I am today. Success isn't supposed to be personal. What is the point of success if there is no one to share it with or no one else shares its benefits? One axiom I've always kept in mind is, 'Success is not determined by how much money you have or how famous you are, but by how many lives you have touched'." This sentiment echoes many of the familiar phrases in the scripture where Jesus talks about what is truly valuable.

Anyone who helped Pat get to where he is today benefitted beyond measure just by knowing him. These benefits extended well beyond the day-to-day interactions we used to have with him. But Pat believed he should not feel good about sharing his success with us, but by sharing his success, he was touching the lives of others. Pat believed in using his platform to benefit meaningful causes and developed a sincere passion for it during his journey. For Pat, he thought that the best way to do this was by starting a foundation to carry out that mission. He created With Us Foundation to help disadvantaged children and make them feel as though they are part of a team. He named the foundation "With Us" to express his desire to bring people together to benefit kids who would have an impact on the next generation. I told Pat that one of my core beliefs is that Coach God is always with us and God's love embraces us all. Pat is a living witness to that essential love of our neighbor in action! How appropriate that he chose the name With Us as he thought of how to "use the scenarios in my life to build this foundation on."

Pat always enjoyed seeing the look on little kids' faces when they get something as simple as a high five from someone "famous." He said, "The expressions and happiness you see in a kids' face when they get an opportunity to do something they thought they would never be able to do is priceless. Now couple that with being a child who is already behind the eight ball due to situations they can't control then you will see what happiness really is." The other side of the foundation deals with the effects of health challenges on children and their families. Pat experienced this firsthand as his younger cousin, Robert Terry Jr. (a.k.a. Bobby Tremendous), was diagnosed with pediatric brain cancer shortly before his third birthday. As a young kid at the time, Pat noticed not only Bobby's "toughness beyond belief and a resiliency many cannot even imagine," but also the difficulties his families and siblings had to go through. "Obviously, I want the With Us Foundation to help the children fighting these diseases, but I want to take it a step further as well. Whether it is providing opportunities and experiences kids could only dream of having or simply being able to deliver Christmas presents to a family who can't afford them due to medical bills, I want to help these families feel like there is another family who cares about them. At the end of the day, if I know there are young adults out there pursuing their dreams because of their hard work and determination, coupled with a helping hand in With Us, then this foundation will be the most satisfying achievement I could accomplish." Given Pat's humility, self-sacrifice, and devotion to those in need, one could see him as a modern-day saint. He certainly lives the message of Jesus and effortlessly executes Coach God's game plan. The mystery of how to live this way was revealed to him by mentors like Coach Graham. Yet I have never heard Pat talk explicitly about God, his play and actions are what bear witness to his faith.

There is one particular basketball moment that millions of people witnessed during March Madness that I refer to as St. Pat's Day. In this scene taken right out of Coach God's playbook, Pat executed the game plan to perfection, even though like all saints, his play was not perfect. The stage for this morality play is one of the biggest, March Madness. It was set the previous summer when Pat sent a message to the team that they needed to listen to his fellow captain Jerian and show up for pickup games. Pat spent a lot of time and effort, before he left to play professional baseball that year, trying to get teammates to communicate openly and not take things personally on the court. This work continued upon his return in the fall. The team also spent a lot of time hanging out together. Team lifts, competitive shooting, pickup games, and philanthropic work all helped the team to gel. The critical moment came when Pat and Jerian met and conveyed to the team that "winning is the most important thing." Now this may not seem appropriate in a book for parents, coaches, and players of youth sports, but in a world where children are encouraged to pursue individual goals at a younger age, their take on it makes sense. Everyone on the team had personal goals. If they pursued their individual goals separately, they were less likely to achieve them. At their level, winning and the public's attention that comes with it has value. If they worked together instead of separately, they were actually more likely to realize their personal goals. So they shared their personal goals so that everyone knew who and what they were fighting for. As Pat said, "This became the key to their season, fight for your brothers in the locker room and fight to win."

Fast-forward to their game against Butler in 2015. The winner would advance to the Sweet Sixteen. Pat was not having a good offensive game (Remember, saints aren't perfect!). Tensions were high. Notre Dame got a defensive stop in a tie game with approximately thirty seconds to go. Zach Auguste secured the rebound, but instead of finding a guard to transition the ball, he tried to dribble down the floor himself, eventually travelling and giving Butler the ball back with three seconds left and a shot to win the game. Butler called time-out. One player started yelling at Zach and telling him he lost the game, things of that nature. In Pat's account, "He calmed him down and told Zach he did not cost us anything, and we needed him to continue our March run. I was able to just genuinely talk to him and explain that this next play, this defensive stop we were about to get, was going to give us our second life, sending it into overtime. That will be your time to help us win this game, and that last play will mean nothing in the grand scheme of anything."

Coming out of the time-out, Butler ran a play to get their best three-point shooter open. Jerian and Pat actually switched on the screen, and the Butler player beat Pat to the spot (Saints aren't perfect). Pat remembered thinking, *This kid is going to hit this shot if he gets it off, and I'm going to have to watch a 'One Shining Moment' happen if that's the case.* Pat was able to recover and came out of nowhere to block his shot, flying through the air and sending the ball into the stands. The video went viral. Notre Dame got the stop they needed and went on to win the game in overtime. The result was, "We stuck together, we put winning above personal goals, and we continued to do what we had set out to do, change the culture of Notre Dame basketball in March. And we did it together."

Why do I call this St. Pat's Day? Upon examination, he overcame personal failings and exhorted his teammates that one mistake does not define a person. He brought a community together to work for a singular purpose. He changed the culture of a community in March, just as the Season of Lent is an opportunity for us to be transformed individually and collectively each spring. Despite his mistakes, he came out of nowhere to give his friends a second life. More than this, he did it all with the same humility that he had learned since his time at Fidelity House. Saints aren't perfect, but I don't know of a better person for a young athlete to look up to than the player Coach God drafted when he created St. Pat!

9

As Luck Would Have It

Some of my students do not believe in God so they certainly do not believe in imagining God as a metaphorical coach or that God is involved in sports in any way. To these students, I always give the advice offered by a former student who was a self-proclaimed atheist as a freshman and only came to know God as a post-graduate philosophy student at USC. He advised, "Tell them to remain open to the possibility and to not think they were the first and only one to ever think that." On the opposite end of the spectrum are the students who have a more "magical" understanding of faith. One student told me he believed in God because when he was playing Little League, he came up to bat with two outs. With the game on the line, he prayed to God to help him. "I remember those days, but I was always praying not to strike out, which I did often, and to escape humiliation. I could hardly conceive of the exhilaration of a walk off hit to win the game." That is exactly what happened for this student-athlete. He had an extra base hit that scored the tying and winning runs and was swarmed in the walk off celebration by his teammates. He was a Little League Big Papi.

So I asked him, "Do you think God didn't like the other team or you prayed harder than that pitcher?" He wasn't sure of his response so I let him ponder the question.

Faith is not magical thinking. We cannot control the humans around us, nor can we control all events in sports. Most of all, we can't control Coach God. Faith is a response to that person and entering into the mystery of that enduring personal relationship. This relationship is not based on luck or pure chance, but is also not empirically quantifiable or subject to the rules of probability. It is even more dangerous when children use prayer magically to pray for an ill relative or friend, thinking we can control not only winning and losing, but suffering and death also. When their prayers are not successful, they lose faith or worse. If they forgot to pray or perform some ritual, they blame themselves. This must always be challenged.

Some people gamble on sports hoping for a lucky payday. Pascal's gamble would be more appropriate. Gamble that Coach God exists, that God cares about you, that God is with you no matter what, and that God has expectations of you. This is a low-risk endeavor because if one is wrong, one won't lost anything! But because winning can seem so daunting or losing so frightening, we put more faith in pre-game rituals, superstitious objects, and symbols all in an attempt to control outcomes and make us feel more secure and confident that we can indeed determine our collective fate as players and fans. Sports managed to fill the gap as religion has become demystified in an age of technology and individualism. When we are fans or on a team, we experience something greater than ourselves. We are filled with hope and anticipation. Whenever the New England Patriots were in the Super Bowl and the fourth quarter was winding down, my family members would say, "Cross your fingers, your toes, your legs, and your butt cheeks!" which, of course, was impossible. But the point was to do everything you can to help your team win, which they often did!

Did we really think that sitting in our exact same seats as the previous successful playoff game, wearing our lucky shirt or sweatshirt no matter how weathered, or eating the same foods could affect the outcome of the game? Of course we did! It made us feel good. We achieved it together. We used to have a saying posted in our locker room, "Luck is when preparation meets opportunity." The Patriots don't win because of our rituals or our superstitions. To even become a professional football player, one needs both luck and talent. These are the ingredients for Coach God's situational football. Then one needs a community dedicated to a singular purpose, like the Patriots. They win because their coaches and their players study, practice, and execute when the situation presents itself. People around these parts worship Bill Belichick and Tom Brady. While Coach God has always emphasized the need for a Sabbath instead of "no days off," their humility and work ethic is something to be emulated by all coaches and athletes.

My view of prayer in sports changed recently, especially after talking to former NFL great, Mark Bavaro. Mark was both praised and criticized for kneeling down and blessing himself after every touchdown he scored as a premier NFL tight end. Winning the Super Bowl twice and displaying his faith publicly for the world to see led to a paradoxical convergence of fame and faith. Every Christian group wanted a piece of him and to claim him as one of their own. Mark experienced a spiritual awakening through his associations with born-again Christians. Who wouldn't want a handsome superstar who also happened to be a faith-filled Christian unafraid to express his faith as a role model for their children? Mark was also criticized for this public display of faith. I did not know about Mark's ritual practice of kneeling down and blessing himself until recently. If I did, I would have been one of the critics. Such displays have always seemed inauthentic to me or they can be an attempt to "score points" with God. That is, until I talked to Mark.

Prayer takes many pathways and forms but is generally a response to the mystery of God in our lives, and it is unique to our situation in life. As Mark asserted, "What farmer doesn't pray for the success of his crops? I would pray just as hard if I worked in a machine shop." Mark's prayer was born out of love for his teammates, for success to be able to provide for his family, and for himself and his own health. He petitioned God to let him play well and long enough to take care of his family. Coach God became coach and also trainer as God healed Mark from his injuries and served as a comfort station along an athletic journey with ups and downs. As a fan, my prayer is more superstition than an expression of faith. Mark's was authentic. I had not considered being a professional athlete as a vocation comparable to being a husband or a father. Mark responded to that call with faith. Like all people, Mark prayed for what he needed, and when he experienced success, he thanked God publicly for all to see. He didn't do it for himself. People, teammates, and family is not enough. We need help from Coach God. Furthermore, Mark would make the sign of the cross as he blessed himself in his humble genuflection of thanksgiving. He would literally take a knee as athletes often do as a sign of respect for their coach.

I attended a baptism yesterday. As the priest traced the sign of the cross on young Timothy's forehead, he asked us to imagine how many times we would make that universal sign of our discipleship to Jesus throughout the course of our lives. Additionally, in times of stress, believers resort to their default setting, which is usually a memorized prayer like an Our Father or a sign of the cross. These are both default settings for all Christians who ask God to be with us in times of stress while also praying, "Thy will be done." That is why Notre Dame's Coach Gerry Faust would go up and down the sidelines exhorting Mark and his teammates to implore God's help during critical moments. People need not be apologetic for blessing themselves publicly. This could be saying grace in a restaurant, on a court or athletic field, or by wearing outward signs of our humility and need for God like ashes. Thank God Mark blessed himself and bore witness to the reality of God in his life so publicly. This takes courage, as does all public witnesses. Disciples can be paralyzed by their own sense of inadequacy and sinfulness. Other people may know their failings and see them as hypocrites. Mark became withdrawn and overwhelmed by both the positive and negative attention he received as a Catholic Christian athlete. Isn't this exactly why we attend worship on Sundays? We fail to live up to our own ideals, to be perfect as Coach God is perfect.

I love the penitential rite at Mass because it reminds me weekly of my inadequacy and need for God in my life. We ask others to pray for us because we are sinners. Luckily, we have people in our communities and families who believe in us even when we don't believe in ourselves. For many athletes, this is a coach. Mark had this experience with legendary coach, Bill Parcells. During training camp, Mark ran a seam pattern and caught a touchdown. When he returned to the huddle, Coach Parcells came up to him and said, "That's the way to go, kid." He slapped his butt then he added, "And you looked good doing it!"

That was when Mark decided he wanted to play for him. Mark told me, "Coach Parcells made me believe I was better than I was until I was that good."

A great coach does that. The coach brings out the best in us and helps us overcome our anxieties, fears, and inadequacies. They believe in us. So does Coach God. God believes in us especially when we don't have the courage to believe in ourselves. This presents an awesome responsibility to our youth coaches! How will our young people come to know God's love and enter into the mystery of that relationship? Their prayer before team meals may be the only *grace* they may ever know. If their coach leads them in expressing thanks, this may be their only experience of Eucharist. Winning can make them egotistical and losing can crush them, unless their coach helps them enter into the mystery of winning and losing. Their postgame handshake is their sign of peace with their opponents after playing a violent game. Their note to an injured friend or hospital visit is the expression of God's healing power. The friendship they form out on the field, on the sideline, or on the bench is a true expression of community. We are the expression of Coach God's love for them as much as the priest of the past.

One of my fellow coaches was orphaned at a young age. His coach took him in, and his family raised him as part of the family. Rather than rail against any movement from religion to sports as a new religious expression, we should embrace it and take hold of this awesome opportunity we have to help young people come to know Coach God through their relationship with us.

1 0

The Life of Bryan

When I was growing up in the 1960s, there was an emphasis on salvation and the doctrine of original sin. I was concerned not only about my own salvation but also that of others. I even thought I needed to convert my college roommate, Dave Kozak, from the National Polish Catholic Church because he didn't believe in papal authority. Thankfully, he was patient with me. We lived together all four years and are still like brothers. I distinctly remember him choosing to wait for me to get back from daily mass to go to dinner instead of going with the rest of our friends. The doctrine of original sin became less important than the reality of brotherly love.

Since then, I have been struck by living examples of original innocence, like someone whose goodness is humbling. I experience this feeling every time I spend time with Bryan Nju-Ghong. I first noticed Bryan while proctoring intramural basketball at our school's outdoor courts. These courts are full of as many as fifty players of all class levels, all sharing only two baskets. Bryan was always welcoming people, making sure they were included, and organizing games in time intervals where no one stayed out too long. Everyone got an opportunity to play. I was so impressed by Bryan's way with people that I interviewed him for a job at our summer camp, Camp Christopher. At the end of the interview, I asked him if someone was picking him up. When he said his mom, I told him I wanted to meet her. I went out to the car and told her that I've never met someone as genuinely nice as Bryan. I said that she had raised him right and thanked her. He later told me that his mother instilled the virtue of humility in him and constantly reminded him that he was blessed. I imagine this is how Mary was with Jesus.

Hiring Bryan was one of the best decisions I have ever made. He often did not go with the other counselors on his break. Instead, Bryan would play with other children. This is how I picture original innocence, just playing and having fun. Too often adults step in, organize, and legislate activities instead of just stepping back and letting children have fun in free play. I had never witnessed such selflessness in twenty-five years of supervising counselors so I asked Bryan why he did this. He said that both at intramural basketball and at camp, he first thought of himself as a counselor and a player but then engaged in divergent thinking to see things in a better way. He started thinking, *What else can I do to have a positive impact on someone's life?* His mother taught him the Golden Rule of Jesus, treat one another as one would like to be treated. So instead of focusing on his own game, he would look around for someone who was not having fun and try to make that person's life better. This was what I witnessed at the outdoor basketball court. He was using his free time to help others with whatever was burdening them at camp. Bryan said he had to distance himself from himself in order to be the servant-leader he wanted to be for others. *Wow!* How did Bryan become like this? Surely his mother, a strong woman of Christian faith, had raised Brian well. But that is not the full story of the life of Bryan.

Bryan's life was not originally innocent. His childhood growing up in Cameroon was tragically changed by the death of his father when he was five. He was then raised and supported by his uncle and mother. They moved to America when he was six. But it was his father that had the most transformative impact on him, even in death. Bryan felt himself being called to be more than he thought he could be. He had heard so many stories of how his dad helped others that he became his moral role model. Bryan set out to honor his father's life by trying to be as good as he is, similar to a youth player emulating a professional or a young coach striving to be like the sagacious veteran. But for Bryan, this was like dream-chasing his father's goodness. He could see him but he was so far ahead, it was like shooting for the stars. The more he moved forward, the farther away it seemed, like something he would never grasp. A child will grow weary and stop chasing his dad if he seemed too far ahead to catch up. But as a young man, Bryan kept striving to reach the level of goodness of his father. He believes he will one day reach that level and will never stop growing in holiness even though it gets harder as he grows older. But Bryan will never become as Coach God. He shared with me his insight into God's coaching style and played according to the Golden Rule.

Bryan believes that assistant coaches like his dad teach what they know until the player is at the same level as the coach. It is similar to the aspiring young athlete moving to professional sports. Sure, there are always things to learn but pretty much every professional athlete is at a different level in ability than the rest of us, although they are at a similar level with each other. Bryan's dad is still teaching him what he needs to do to be as good as he can be but eventually, he will be alongside him as a colleague. His teacher will be God's Spirit, who alone is all good and teaches us the wisdom that comes from God alone. At that point, his father and mother will be companions on the same journey led by the head coach, Coach God. As a parent, I found this difficult myself, figuring out when to let go and let God guide my son and daughter beyond my capabilities. Altogether, God wants us to be free and to have life abundantly. The more Bryan plays by the Golden Rule, the freer he becomes, the closer to his goal, and the more the others around him become free.

Bryan's uncle and mother contributed to Bryan's freedom in specific ways. In Cameroon, Bryan's uncle used to bring him to soccer games. Bryan is a tremendous athlete and played lacrosse and basketball at our school, but his first love is soccer. Bryan described soccer as a game where one can be totally free, relax, and have fun while taking in the total sensory experience of the grass and smells of warm weather. For Bryan, soccer is a spiritual experience, allowing him to "soak in the presence of God" as he is having fun. This is his vision of sport and play. While I also imagine this is what Coach God wants for us, Bryan not only imagines it, he lives it. There isn't the apprehension of violent collisions like in football or lacrosse or some of the ego that has become emphasized in basketball with dribble-drive offenses and three-point shooting dominating the game. Bryan longed to play against his uncle in Cameroon but he was too young. Since coming to America, he found there is more stress from many different angles than there was in Cameroon. Soccer provides an even more valued spiritual oasis where Bryan can connect with God and not think about anything else except enjoying the game. He had his uncle to thank for introducing him to soccer. Hopefully he will be able to play with him some day in Cameroon.

The spiritual freedom Bryan's mother provided was of a different sort. Bryan's father was Catholic and his mother a Protestant. Upon his death, his mother continued to bring Bryan to a Catholic church. As an African Catholic, sometimes it was a struggle to find a church that nurtured Bryan's spiritual life in a way the Catholic church in Cameroon did. Luckily, Bryan and his mother found a Cameroonian Catholic church in Salem, Massachusetts, that celebrates Jesus in a way that is more consonant with Bryan's experience of God. His celebrations are full of singing, clapping, and movement by which he can feel the spirit doing something in him. Life in America has many stresses. Bryan depended on his church and the Catholic school he attended, St. John's Prep, as a place he can relax and allow himself to be free. With his assistant coach father and supportive mother at his spiritual side, he can let go and let Coach God coach him. He just plays.

11

Why Bad Things Happen to Good Players

It was 2008, we were playing a junior varsity game at Catholic Memorial. On a goal line play one of our linemen, Dan Culkeen, was hurt so I walked out onto the field to see what the trainer had to say. He was eventually helped to the bench where another player, Brandon Coppola, was sitting rather rigidly. I asked him what was wrong, and he said, "My neck hurts if I move it like this."

I told him not to move and yelled across the field for the trainer. At halftime, his mother asked if she could take him home because I was obviously not going to put him in. I agreed. On the way home, he was feeling so much pain that they decided to go to the emergency room. After examination, they determined that he had broken his neck at the C4 and C5 vertebrae. He was put in a neck brace, and his football career was over. However, his two triplet brothers, Tyler and Jared, continued playing. On the Friday before Labor Day 2009, Jared was playing outside linebacker in a scrimmage against Lynn English at the Manning Bowl in Lynn. There was a collision, and Jared fell to the ground.

As he lay there motionless, he became keenly aware of God's presence. "I was lying on my back on the field, and I couldn't feel anything. I thought from that point on, everything is going to be all right. I'll be OK with whatever is going to happen." He wasn't sure what happened and thought he would be fine in a couple of months.

This was grace from God that helped him in the beginning to keep looking forward and keep the mind-set he would be fine. At the hospital, he experienced two more experiences of God's grace. The attending physicians conducted surgery to immediately relieve the pressure on his spinal cord. One also recommended the Shepherd Center in Atlanta, which has proven to be life-changing for Jared and countless other persons with spinal cord or brain injuries. More importantly, while at the hospital, he looked at his mom and he said, "You're not crying. So if you're OK, I know I am going to be OK." Jared's mom Dawn was able to enter into the mystery of Jared's and her suffering as they both embarked on a journey like Job's that continues to this day.

Meanwhile, back at school, we all struggled to make sense of Jared's injury and decided we should pray together. That night, the head coach called me. The headmaster suggested we hold a Mass for Jared on Monday after our next scrimmage and invite parents and players. We had a liturgy every year at Camp Androscoggin where we held our preseason camp. The head coach and I decided that it would be better to pray as we usually did as a team. I would preside over the service. My truest prayers come from my heart even though I enjoy traditional prayers as well as meditation and contemplation. I truly felt in the depths of my being that Jared would walk someday so I composed the following prayer:

Lord, reduce all swelling.
And in our dwelling,
Inflame our hearts with
Love for our brother.
We will not complain
About our pain
Restore feeling to
His limbs again.
Bless the doctors in their skill
Our fearful hearts still
So we can trust that you are Lord.
You are faithful in your Word.

Please to our brother talk
And tell him, "Jared, rise!"
Pick up your mat
And walk.
Amen.

I then found a Museum of Fine Arts painting of the biblical scene of the Pool of Bethesda and made prayer cards for all attendees at the service. I encouraged them to pray daily, as I did. I kept the card in my wallet so that every day when I took out some lunch money, I would be reminded of what was really important in life. I saw the prayer posted on the Internet and heard from a relative states away that they knew people who were also praying the prayer for Jared. The prayers worked! Jared had amazing community support and spent many months at the rehabilitation center in Atlanta, Georgia. One of the most moving moments in my life was seeing him walk across the field on Thanksgiving Day for the coin toss using his walker. It reaffirmed my belief in the power of prayer, or so I thought. I wasn't wrong but I definitely wasn't right either. I had not entered into the mystery of what Coach God was doing with Jared and God's assistant, Dawn. She knew the game plan. I had become a spectator, a cheerleader. She was God's assistant coach! For those who find an image of God as woman problematic, they need only to examine the coaching of Dawn Coppola. Her deep abiding faith has given me renewed insight into our relationship with God, especially when bad things happen to good players. Dawn believes that God knows when we need something. God will put people in our life not in violation of their free will, but in cooperation with the promptings of God's Spirit, *rhua*, a feminine term in the Scriptures for the spirit that gives us life, like God and Dawn gave life to Jared. Like Job of old, Dawn never cursed God for Jared's injury. She knew it was not punishment. They did nothing wrong. She believed that things happen for a reason. Coach God wanted this. It was part of the game plan. She also knew that if anyone could handle it, Jared could.

Jared also came to believe this. He believes that God is good and can bring good things out of suffering. He believes God likes to challenge people who can deal with them and overcome them. Coaches do this in order to get the best out of their athletes and for the team. Spectators often doubt or criticize what they are doing. They don't know. They can't see the broader picture in hopes for a win. Even though I was one of Jared's coaches at the time, I was truly one of these spectators. I wanted to see Jared walking so badly that I was not open to the mystery of prayer and how God works with us. While Jared still works to become stronger and to walk further and more often, this is not his preoccupation. He won't be devastated if that doesn't happen. He could spend all of his time working at this every day and improving his physical conditioning, but that is not what his team needs. It is not why God chose him to suffer a spinal cord injury.

While I was praying for Jared to walk, Dawn and Jared were living the prayer of all Christians, "Thy will be done." I struggle with this prayer because it makes me realize that I don't know for certain what God's will is for anyone. I have enough trouble discerning it for myself. Jared has been living independently for the past year and a half in Atlanta. He continues to overcome tough challenges because he never lived by himself. He moved to Atlanta because on top of his career in finance, he wants to give back to the community that helped him, the Shepherd Center. While he is going through his own journey, he wants to share his story to help inspire others. He volunteers at Shepherd in the peer support group, attends the Adventure Skills Workshop, and helps people experience the life-giving energy of adaptive sports. He and his mom are grateful that his injury was not worse and that he can use it as a gift to help others in similar or worse situations.

Being a spectator of their journey has transformed my view on prayer. While we are encouraged to petition Coach God for what we need, this may be Monday morning quarterbacking in a spiritual sense. Like Dawn Coppola, I believe God knows what we need before we know it. I feel like I should have been praying for Jared to receive whatever he needed, not what I thought he needed. When I would look in my wallet and see the prayer I composed for him, I thought I was praying for what was most important (the win), but this was not what was most important to Jared. His spiritual journey is different than mine, as is the journey of each player. Jared's journey into the mystery of what God is doing with him requires great courage and openness, but it also requires his mother. When I asked Jared about any transformative experience of God's presence, he replied, "My mom. She was down there the whole time. She went home one weekend. I didn't realize how much my parents sacrificed raising kids. When I couldn't do little things, she brushed my teeth and fed me. I don't ever talk about how much my mom …" his voice trailed off. He then said quietly, "My mom is my motivation. She is a big part of where I am today and where I'll be in the future." Her encouragement enabled Jared to move to Atlanta by himself, like a mother pushing her bird out of the nest to take flight on its own.

Dawn marveled at Jared's courage, but it wasn't genetic. Virtues like courage are learned through patient, endurance, and practice again and again. Dawn told Jared to water ski or she wouldn't visit him, so he did! She did the right thing by her sons even when there is reason to be afraid for them. She overcame her own fear with courage and the infused virtues of faith, hope, and love despite the fears she faced as a mother. Brandon broke his neck sophomore year. Then Jared broke the same vertebrae in junior year and was partially paralyzed. Tyler was the third triplet. Was this coincidence? Accident? Genetic defect? Therefore by letting Tyler continue playing as the team's premier running back, was she risking his life and health? Jared insisted that Tyler be able to play his senior year. Dawn realized that she had no control over what was going to happen in Tyler's life. If God wanted it to happen, it would. Coach God knew the game plan. While Jared's injury was accidental, it was not coincidental. By being open to this mystery, everyone benefitted. She let Tyler play what became a record-setting season and trip to the Division 1 Super Bowl. Tyler scored on the first play from scrimmage, but that was the end of the scoring.

Our coach was criticized for not putting the ball in the air enough. Spectators and commentators criticized the game plan. They did not know our quarterback had a shoulder injury that prevented him from throwing. It wasn't in the injury report. The report on Jared from that fateful day was perceived as a tragedy but was actually a gift. He and his mother were certain that he was chosen for this injury. Dawn received external confirmation from Coach God of his abiding presence. Jared is living independently in Atlanta but not by himself. His whole coaching staff is there, encouraging him to put his life "in the air" as he makes a difference in the lives of so many people. Coach God is there, while God's assistant head coach, Dawn and I continue to be spectators, cheering them on. I realize I shouldn't presume the game plan.

12

Sudden Death or Over Time

The mystery of death is as troubling as injury or suffering, yet it can also be a powerful moment of God's grace, whether it is sudden or occurs over time. Any coach who ever had a player die during the season can attest to the power of a team in supporting each other. I experienced this firsthand in my second year at St. John's Prep in 1991. We started off the season with an overtime victory in the first meeting between then number four in the country, Brockton High of Rocky Marciano fame. We had one more game before we would see them again as we tried to complete an undefeated season in the state championship. That last regular season game was held on Thanksgiving in Harvard Stadium against an overmatched Cambridge Rindge and Latin team. We won easily and every senior played so that every parent, coach, and player went home happy to their Thanksgiving gatherings.

However, one of our players, Chip Schreunder, never made the bus. This was before the era of Internet and cell phones so we didn't know until our arrival back at school that Chip, a sophomore scout team player, had been in a car crash on Thanksgiving Eve. His parents decided to take Chip off life support on Friday night. I don't remember much about the funeral the next week until the very end as we, in our blue blazers and khaki pants, lined the driveway around the chapel at Merrimack College. As the hearse passed by, players joined hands in a spontaneous expression of support for Chip's family and each other. Not a word was mentioned but the spirit flowed throughout our bodies from one player to another. I would love to say we went out that week and won the state title for Chip in true "win one for the Gipper" tradition. However, we lost 13–7. Our coach, Jim O'Leary, never believed in dedicating a game to anyone because the price was too high to pay emotionally if you thought you let them down by losing.

The Long Blue Line tradition of forming an honor guard became a Prep tradition and has been present at numerous funerals from that day forward. It is more orchestrated now but still evokes the silent, tearfully mouthed "thank you" from the faces peering out somberly from the cars in the funeral procession as they pass by. That was the last year we played anyone besides Xaverian Brothers High School on Thanksgiving Day. The Thanksgiving game became one of great rivalry, often featuring top teams in the state whose rosters are filled with future collegiate and pro football players. However, the most memorable impact of God's presence was felt around the player who wasn't there. They say you can't coach players if they aren't there referring to player attendance, and that is true, but Coach God can. Coach God and the player are always present to each other, even if the player only pauses to acknowledge this presence on Sundays. I believe Coach God welcomed Chip into an everlasting Thanksgiving postgame gathering where he waits an eternal reunion with his family and teammates.

We are Easter people. We believe in the resurrection of Jesus and the promise of eternal life. This can be difficult to believe in the throes of the grieving process. Just like in sudden death overtime when the end comes, there is a wide range of emotions from celebration to inconsolable tears. The losers feel as if all hope has been crushed and their journey has ended in ultimate defeat. But death is not the ultimate defeat. Our head coach is the only one who can turn what seems like a crushing defeat into eternal victory. Sometimes we even get a glimpse into the reality of this victory.

Every year, our team used to go up to football camp for preseason training. One year while I was at camp, a close friend I assisted coaching youth basketball with had a daughter, Emma, who was fighting cancer at Massachusetts General Hospital. At camp Saturday night, we would have a Eucharistic prayer service every year as a team. This prayer service always contained a Prayer of the Faithful. We invited our football team to mention people in their lives who needed our prayers so we pray for them. I planned on mentioning Emma in this portion of the service that night. I was asleep in my bunk around four in the morning when I suddenly had a vision of Emma lying on a white pillow, smiling, and surrounded by light. I was certain she was transitioning into the afterlife. It was more like a vision than a dream. I can still see it as clearly now as then. I woke up, looked at my flip phone's time, and went back to sleep to await the 5:30 a.m. alarm signaling it was time for conditioning. When that horn woke me from my sleep, I sat on the edge of my bed and started texting my friend Derek that we would pray for Emma during our prayer service. Halfway through my text, I stopped. I knew she already died. It wouldn't be right to pray for her to live. I closed up my phone, and went to practice. At practice, I received a text from Derek that Emma had died. Her whole journey of suffering and death was over. It was so sad to see a child and family suffer through this. At the wake, I told Derek of my vision. He asked me if I could tell his wife, Tina, because one of the things bothering her the most was wondering if her daughter was all right. I told her, but I also prayed that God would reveal this assurance to her instead of me. I still prayed for Emma that night at the prayer service but I prayed mostly for her family, for their healing, and for God to give them whatever they need, including peace. This peace comes at different times for all of us since we all grieve differently. It is not a linear process. But for all of us, it ends in resurrection and a reunion with our loved ones, our teammates, our family, and our friends. We can be certain of this part of the game plan. It is hard to make any sense out of the death of a child. When my niece Clare was living with leukemia, I had a hard time teaching religious studies. The only prayer I could utter was "Lord, have mercy." I would still attend Mass but those were the only words I actually prayed. I never understood her death, but I do have assurance of her living eternally with God.

The night before my family moved to Massachusetts to escape a dangerous situation, she appeared to me at three in the morning as I was sleeping in my brother-in-law's house. In order for the move to happen, five houses had to sell in succession the next day. My realtor asked me if I had any guardian angels. I assured her that I didn't have angels but I knew people who had gone before me interceded for me. Clare appeared to me during that night and said, "I made this move happen for the sake of my cousins. I hope they like the backyard." I woke my wife up to tell her Clare just appeared to me then we went back to sleep. That day, all five houses closed, and we made a move that still influences the course of our family life. I still don't have answers concerning Clare's suffering and death, but I can live in that mystery because I have trust in her eternal life with Coach God.

Sometimes the meaning of suffering and death is partially created by our response in this life. While I was coaching track at Trinity High School in the 1980s, our guidance office received a request for help from a local family. Their child was undergoing chemotherapy in Boston, and the frequent trips to the hospital prevented them from the upkeep of their property. The track team responded by going to the house after practice on successive weekends and doing all of their spring cleanup and yard work. When the child died, they went as a team to the wake to support the family. I was so proud of them! Sometimes God's presence is experienced when God's athletes do something as simple as showing up and becoming God's loving presence to someone who needs tangible support. They never met the child themselves, but I know the family not only appreciated their work, but also their loving presence in the midst of their tremendous loss.

As I wrote this chapter, my mother-in-law, Carol Christian LaPointe, was being sent home from the hospital to live out her final days in the comfort of her home. My mother-in-law accepted me into her family and loved me as her son. It is hard to go through the daily anticipatory grieving process as an individual and as a family. Players cannot enter a game thinking they will lose, even though they know it is a fifty-fifty proposition. When I think of postgame talks I or other coaches have given after tough losses, they all feel empty and wanting. I don't like to say much after a loss. What good is there to say? I would rather let myself feel its sting. That is why one of my favorite lines in scripture is also the shortest, "And Jesus wept." Jesus was moved over the death of his friend, Lazarus. He ended up winning the ultimate victory by overcoming the power of death and restoring Lazarus to life, but he let himself feel the loss first. Jesus showed us a glimpse into his power as Son of God and he also showed us what it means to be fully human!

At some Catholic funerals, I feel that we spend too much time in our head and not enough time in our hearts, especially if too many words are being said by a priest who does not know the deceased. The application of the theological import of the story of Jesus matters less to me than the eulogy courageously offered by a loved one. I would much prefer to share the stories and memories of the person just like my high school team used to gather on postgame Saturday nights, play billiards, and recount all of the little side stories that happened during the game. I had to give a eulogy for my student, Sean Souza. Sean used to come over to my house to watch Celtics versus Lakers playoff games when the Celtics had their original Big Three and the Lakers had Magic Johnson and Kareem Abdul-Jabbar. I loved the Celtics; he loved Kareem. As a matter of fact, he used to often talk about his desire to meet the star someday. Unfortunately, Sean died just after receiving a potentially life-saving liver transplant. During the eulogy, I noted that I could not escape his suffering. His life was one marked by suffering. He could never make it to school before eleven thirty due to illness, and often missed class. Yet through my friendship with this young man whose life was marked with suffering, he was able to become my teacher about courage, humility, joy, and hope. The truth is the story of Jesus' passion, death, and resurrection matters! At the time, this truth may not touch our hearts, and it may not make our grieving any easier. But instead of seeing death, either sudden or not, as the end of the game, over time, if we enter into the mystery of the game plan, we will come to know the ultimate victory in our hearts where God's game plan is ultimately revealed.

13

The Gospel According to John

I have heard a lot of playbooks referred to as the Bible or the Gospel, but nothing could be further from the truth. The Bible is not a play-book for executing plays with precision that lead you to the prom-ised land via something akin to a Hail Mary pass. The Bible is an inspiring collection of writings of various genres, including wisdom, historical accounts, poetry, and, most of all, stories that capture the imagination. These stories, more than any moral norm or carefully crafted deductive syllogism, help us to engage in the mystery of who God is and who we are called to be in response to God's love. The process of figuring out in the practical reality of day-to-day living is called discernment. When it comes to sports, no one has demon-strated more clearly to me God's presence on earth in athletics than Coach John Barbati. He taught me to live according to the Gospel of John.

In the Gospel of John, historical narrative carries great impor-tance. He is eighty-five years young, and still coaching football (Massachusetts) and baseball (Florida). He can tell stories of the fabled Everett football program from seventy years ago when they used to roll up newspapers to use as shoulder pads to play other towns on Sundays. I remember one particular story in Everett Village Sandlot football one Sunday. While in Roxbury playing a well-equipped uniformed team, the Roxbury coach at the half was heard shout-ing, "These raggedy Everett boys are beating us with their underwear on!" John takes great pride in telling us of how they won on that day and on many other Sundays growing up in Everett. His stories connect him to a legacy of pride in his community that continues today. Oftentimes competitive athletics become arrogant in the drive to be better than an individual opponent, a team, or a community. That is not the sort of pride John bears for his community. John definitely promotes a competitive model of sports. He coached some of the absolute best players in the country, including now famous baseball players: Johnny Damon, A.J. Pierzynski, Brian Barber, and Dan Miceli; and NFL players, Jack Concannon, Arthur Graham, Mark Roopinian, and Brian St Pierre. But his model of competition bred humility, not arrogance. "If you are the best, prove it," John would say. Reality should not be clouded with excuses, laziness, politics, or anything else that detracts from pure competition. This is one of the ways God speaks to me through John. He demands the best out of players but he also sees the goodness in them. If one cannot comprehend a play today, he promises that tomorrow they will be better. In staff meetings when coaches would wonder if a player could perform their job, he would say not to worry about it. He'll do it. If he can't, it is our job to teach him until he can!

I am far too judgmental to ever be like John. I have been willing to close the book too soon on a developing player when I became frustrated. The grace the player has available to them that day is enough for John. Tomorrow they will be better. Don't worry about tomorrow; today has enough concerns of its own. As a result of his care and encouragement (and extremely knowledgeable coaching), they will be better. Sounds a lot like Coach God, doesn't it? I have never heard him use sarcasm, profanity, a put-down, or anything that would discourage a player, except to point out their own lack of effort. I believe this is how God deals with us—or at least I hope it is. God challenges us to be our best, not pausing too long to chastise us for our failings but encourages us to be better. God gives us the grace to enable us to do what he calls us to do, but also consoles us when our ignorance or frailty keeps us from realizing our true potential.

Like Coach God, John is about naming the truth. If you are in a one-on-one blocking drill against someone competing for a starting spot and you win, you start. There is no ambiguity. John sees the potential in everyone, from the young coach to the aspiring ten-year-old. Everyone is good and is going to get better if they work at it. John is the director of a skills camp for young children. He is small in stature, a combination of a Yoda and an Elmer Fudd-type character. However, he demands your attention. If he is talking to you one-on-one, he will often grab your wrist as if to say, "Don't pull away. I want to talk to you." In this age when we are reluctant to touch one another, John pulls the person he is talking to in, much like God does in prayer to make us pay attention. Then he communicates immortal words of wisdom with things like, "Twenty years from now people won't remember that play, but they will remember you and whether you were a good teammate." He taught my son that when he was ten years old in his skills camp, and it truly stuck with him. I have heard stories from his college teammates of how he stood up for them and against others when they were being accosted with racial epithets. I witnessed him do the same thing while playing high school football. This year, a parent of one of his teammates approached me and told me how my son sent their son out of the huddle because he didn't seem right. He ended up being diagnosed with a concussion. They were grateful that my son noticed something was wrong, sparing their son from further brain injury. More than any sermon he heard in church or moral maxim he learned at St. John's Prep, this teaching about being a good teammate shaped his character as he made his way through the world of sports. He never read it but he certainly took to heart the preaching from the Gospel of John!

I see John on the sidelines at games even when his team isn't even playing. He is often wearing a red-and-black hunter's coat that only exaggerates his Elmer Fudd resemblance. What is he doing there? He is enjoying the pure love of the sport, lost in his element. Sometimes I worry he is going to be run over by a player going out of bounds. Now nearing ninety years old, he is not as nimble as he once was, although he still has more energy than I do! I have never seen him asked to leave the sidelines by an official, a coach who doesn't know who he is or even an opposing coach. I have even seen him coach another team's opposing players just for the love of the game and purity of the sport. (I don't think our opponents knew, and it certainly wasn't meant in a malicious way.) If John sees someone doing something incorrectly, he assumes he may not have been taught. He wants them to have their best chance at success so he shares his knowledge and wisdom with them. In that moment, the player is not our opponent, he is our neighbor and John loves him as such. Even though his instruction might cost us the game, it is irrelevant. I believe God made football players, that they were born to play football, and Coach God created John to coach them.

What I most admire about John is he always tells the truth. He is realistic with both players and parents. He can't even be fired anymore. He is a Hall of Famer in two states and doesn't even want pay. He volunteers! I suppose you can't really fire God either, although you can stop talking to God or tune out what you don't want to hear. In the Jesuit process of discernment, besides listing pros and cons and becoming aware of consolations and desolations, one process is to imagine what someone you admire would do. When it comes to coaching, I don't imagine what God would do or Jesus would say. WWJD means for me "what would John do" or say in this situation? Will I be proud of the body of my life's work if I take this job or compromise on this principle? John's example inspires me to be my best self, although I don't always succeed. I'll bet most people reading this book have someone like John who modeled how God wants us to be in sports. Indeed, most of us encounter God in the people we interact with every day. I felt a little presumptuous writing this book as if I could know how God would coach until I realized I really do know. God would and does coach like Coach John.

1 4

Passing the Baton

I love coaching track and field. The difference one can make in a young athlete's life is so rewarding. Every day they come to practice, trying to achieve a measurable personal best. It may be as small as an increment of a quarter of an inch in a long jump or one second in an eight-hundred-meter run, but it means the world to that athlete. It keeps them going. In a sport so measured by individual accomplishments, it remains a very collegial sport. Athletes have lots of times to socialize and form friendships. Coaches, while competitive, also want other teams' athletes to compete well. When one wins, one knows one has beaten someone's best. They can also leave the venue feeling good about themselves because they ran the best race of their lives even though they may have come in second, or last. As a result, some of the moral exemplars I hold in coaching are track and field coaches at St. John's Prep. As Coach Jack Klein said in a recent faculty meeting, "We need to keep our integrity as evaluators and parents need to trust us." These men are known to have impeccable integrity and passed on not only their knowledge gained from years of experience and study regarding the physics of track and field, but also their wisdom of how to be with young athletes as well.

Some events in track are also team events. In the four-by one-hundred-meter relay, four sprinters sprint a hundred meters each around the track, seamlessly passing a baton. After finishing their legs, the first three runners watch from afar, rooting for their teammate to finish the race strong. This group of four individuals are practicing every day, marking their steps, and trying to get the perfect timing. When done correctly, the passes flow effortlessly as the relay team transitions through the race. But when catastrophe happens, it can leave the individuals involved and the team rattled.

I was part of such a catastrophe. One year, I was assigned to work with the relay team. We were at the state meet, and the runner of the third leg of the race was approaching the passing zone, a marked area of the track where the passing of the baton is allowed. If one passes the baton too soon or too late, one is disqualified. I watched eagerly as the penultimate runner entered the zone. Our anchor runner, Josh Nicholson, started to take off, accelerating through the zone. Then something happened. I can't remember what exactly. Did he slow down? Did the runner run up his back? Did he take off too soon? All I know is I can still hear the baton rattling on the track as it dropped to the ground. I, equally rattled, felt like dropping to the ground too. I felt like I let them down, that I had failed. Perhaps I did not drill them enough. I was filling in for the usual sprint coach that season and he always had us in the top five relays in the state. There were no words of consolation I could offer to Josh or the rest of the relay team. There were no *do-overs*. This event ended his senior season.

Life is like that. Sometimes things don't go as planned, and we don't get a do-over. Fortunately, track is not life. Unless we are dead, we always have a chance to practice virtue again and to successfully pass on what we have learned to another. Jared Coppola learned that after becoming paralyzed. He wrote to me about the relationship he developed with another student, Trey. Even though Jared can still only walk a hundred meters at a time, he handed off his spiritual baton of selflessness to Trey to continue the race. He wrote, "Trey was a Northeastern cooperative student who began his internship when I started my therapy at Boston Medical Center. He worked with me three times per week. When his internship ended and he graduated, he took a position in the clinic and continued to work with me for the next year and a half. His mother contacted my mom and expressed to her how inspired Trey was from working with me and meeting us. Trey is now attending school to become a physical therapist. He lives in Colorado and working at one of the top spinal cord injury rehab hospitals. Being around him during those two years helped me through a difficult time. At the same time, I was able to help guide him to where he is today."

One of our football and baseball coaches tells the players the story of how he was a ward of the state when he was a young boy. He had a conflict over a curfew in his foster home and was going to run away. Forty of his teammates found him at a local restaurant. With his coach, he went back to the house to try reaching a peaceful resolution to the crisis. His coach went into the foster home and offered to take Dick Phillips in if they could not resolve the conflict. With the support of his team and coach, he had the courage to work things out with his foster family. Coach Phillips tells this story to emphasize the importance of one's team as a secondary family. He always appreciated that his coach was willing to take him into his home. Coach Phillips was a decorated sprinter in his day. He knew about passing the baton. However, his best pass came in his work as a trustee in Hillside School. Coach Phillips lived at this orphanage as a child and spent decades tirelessly working to pass on loving guidance and acceptance to today's orphans. He learned this generosity from his coach. Passing it on is the embodiment of Coach God who commanded us to be mindful of the orphans in our midst.

Coach John Barbati passed the baton (his wisdom) to more coaches than I can count. In the early spring of 1950, while working as a helper on a soda delivery truck in Everett, a total stranger came up to the truck and asked him if his name was John Barbati and if he would like to go to college! He excitedly jumped off the truck and asked, "Where?"

He answered, "St. Michael's College."

"Where's that?"

The stranger then explained the conditions to qualify for an athletic scholarship. John qualified academically but had to qualify athletically each year. John's father insisted that he not go and that he should learn to be a bricklayer or a stonemason. Eventually, his mother and older brother convinced his father to allow him to go, especially since it would cost the family nothing except incidental expenses. St. Michael's College provided an opportunity for John to pursue his love of sports. He was inducted into the Hall of Fame not only at St. Michael's College, but in Massachusetts as well. He also had the field in Florida where he coached such greats as Johnny Damon and A. J. Pierzynski named after him. The wisdom he passed on is recounted in chapter ten, but others also passed on their love of sports by donating to provide the opportunity for him to pursue his dreams in athletics and education. Ironically, John became a resident assistant at St. Michael's College his senior year. One of his freshman charges was a young scholar, a basketball player named Tom Lovett. They recently reunited while my son Sean who was playing in the Massachusetts Shriners game. John started this game as a way of using football to raise money to heal the lame, crippled, and burned children of our country. As I said, he passed on more batons than anyone I know.

I would be remiss if I did not mention my father as the prior leg in my relay. I decided not to become a priest in part because I saw how he served Coach God through his interactions with his players. When I played basketball as a teenager all day at the town basketball courts in Wolfeboro, New Hampshire, adult men would come up to me and tell me what my father had done for them. He didn't just coach them, he listened to them and got to know them as people first and athletes second. As a son, I tried to model myself after him much as Bryan Nju-Ghong strived to emulate his father. My father was never much of a sprinter. As a matter of fact, now he can barely walk. But he did have a memorable hundred-yard walk. He coached at several schools in New Hampshire and Vermont in his career, usually revitalizing programs. When I was a young boy in the early 1960s, he coached at Bellows Falls High School. Springfield High School was a big rival, which I remember because I got in an argument with a Springfield boy that year about which school was better! In 1989, the tables had turned, and he had a remarkable group of seniors preparing for this rivalry game. On the last day of practice, he had the seniors gather under the goal posts at one end of the field. He spaced underclassmen and coaches every five yards down the field and beyond. Each senior walked up to each player, and each player spoke personally to them, mostly in appreciation for where they led us. It was a very sacred moment, like an extended sign of peace at the Eucharistic celebration. I borrowed this idea for the last practice of our 1997 state championship team, and it was equally as moving. It was a great way to honor our departing seniors as they passed the baton to us, the underclassmen. Moreover, as a coach, I called my father with difficult situations I faced in coaching when I wasn't sure what to do. He was always spot on with his advice, faithfully passing the wisdom he gained to me and my athletes. Whenever I am faced with a situation, I think *WWJD*. That is, what would John do? These two men are the epitome of Coach God's relay team in my life.

I am grateful to have these mentors in my life. I realize that not everyone is so fortunate. Coach God does not leave us orphans. God takes us in as Coach Phillips' coach offered to take him in. In the Scriptures, the Father ran the first leg, Jesus ran the second leg (although in Roman Catholic, tradition it is more like a *filioque* three-legged race), and the Holy Spirit took what Jesus passed on and has handed it off to us. We are the anchor leg. Not for everyone, but for someone. When we finish our race, we are called to hand over what is truly of God to future generations, future coaches, and athletes. We are all called to hand over what we know is true and good in sport, to make a seamless pass of the baton. One knows how good this can be when one sees another runner stop and help an injured runner cross the finish line together. We know this goodness can overcome evil as it does every year through the spirit of the Boston Marathon. Remember Steve Langton of the Amazing Race? He ran the 4x100 relay in high school. We all run the amazing race in life, except we always cross the finish line together with our fellow runners. They are not cheering from afar; they are right with us—the Father, the Son, and the Holy Spirit!

15

Hope for the Future

Coaches coach, players play, and parents parent. All three relationships have to be right in order for us to grow spiritually and increase in virtue as we participate in sports. However, we should add one other axiom, believers *believe*! I have come to understand that all an athlete needs to be successful is one person to believe in them. This person does not need to be the same person for everyone on a team. For many of us, it is our mothers or fathers.

Early in our marriage, my wife read a book that claimed a daughter's confidence is directly linked to her relationship with her father. I never forgot this. She chose to stay at home and work six hours a day so someone was always home for the kids. I was busy teaching; coaching football, basketball, and track; running a summer camp; and serving as intramurals director. For nine years, I commuted an hour or more to work so I rarely saw the children awake until weekends. My son even said one weekend, "Thanks for coming to see me at my house today, Dad." I told him I lived there, but he said, "No, you are never home." So even though coaching was a financial necessity and I could not embark on his guilt trip, I made sure my time at home was quality time.

For sons playing football, their mothers are the ones who often believe in them. Some didn't even understand the game but they went anyway to support their sons My first boss, Virginia Bailey Skelley, was more than that. I spent most of my youth playing basketball in her backyard for hours on end. Whenever there was a Celtics playoff game, the neighbors would gather at her house to cheer on the Big Three. I never knew until her four sons eulogized her at her memorial service how much her support in football meant to them. Each one told the same story. After each game, she would greet them, hug them, and tell them, "Great job! You were the best one out there," even when they weren't. This meant a lot to them. It means a lot to us also if we can only hear the word of Coach God telling us the same thing. Our fathers may believe in their sons, but they can also influence them negatively. I have seen many players play football because their dad wants them to. Unfortunately, if they don't really want to play and feel they had to in order please their dads, they often shy away in contact drills, which is a dangerous situation for them. If they would like to try a violent contact sport like football but their mothers will not allow it, this also can prevent them from achieving their best. Any hesitancy on the part of the mother is often linked to fears of injury, especially concussions. Not everyone is meant to play such physical games. These fears are legitimate, but concussions can also be acquired in other ways. My daughter received a concussion when someone threw a basketball across the gym and hit her head, which hit the bleachers as she walked through the gym on the way to lacrosse practice. In summer camp, some children had concussions playing soccer and landing on the turf. We cannot let these fears paralyze us if our sons or daughters want to play a contact sport.

We know the unbreakable bond between a mother and her son. Fathers hope for us; mothers believe in us. It shouldn't surprise anyone that in Jesus' hour of need, it was his mother and mostly women at the foot of the cross. Most of the men left in fear. It also isn't surprising that he revealed his resurrection to Mary Magdalene in all four gospels. She also believed in him but when she told the apostles, they didn't believe her or in him. They were still filled with fear until Pentecost, the coming of the Holy Spirit. For others, their confidence comes from their coach, usually an assistant coach. The head coach expresses confidence in the starters, as is obvious from them being placed in a starting role, but the assistant coach is the one that advocates for the individual player in staff meetings. They let the player prove themselves and be successful in individual drills. The assistant coach also has the ability to pull an athlete aside during the school day in a classroom or in the halls and check in with a player. One such meeting was with a player named Dan Riley.

Dan was an undersized linebacker with a big heart. We developed a relationship through sports and class. Dan would confide in me if he had any troubles at home. Sometimes he would even come over to my apartment to talk. During his junior year, Dan was preparing to quit football. He wasn't playing much and didn't really get along with the head coach. We talked at length about whether he would have any regrets if he quit. Dan stuck it out even though the head coach was upset with him for thinking of quitting. Luckily, Dan had an opportunity to go in on defense since the team had a good lead on our opponent. He had an unbelievable sense that he was to do something different. Dan was sent in at middle linebacker but switched himself to outside linebacker. As he heard some of the coaches yelling at him for switching, the ball was snapped. Dan dropped to his zone, read the play, and cut in front of the intended receiver. He intercepted the pass and returned it for a touchdown. He was subsequently swarmed by his teammates and was held up as a role model by the head coach after the game. "We need more players like Dan Riley," he said.

Dan never forgot this. In fact, he viewed it as a miracle. When he wrote to me about this event, he said he looked at me like I saved his life. He believed that his decision to not quit football allowed Coach God to provide a miracle. Dan expressed that this miracle reminded him that he is loved and capable of great things in life. He vowed that day to make the best of his life with the gifts that God gave him. Dan is almost fifty now. He is working with young people as a substance abuse counselor and high school counselor. He devotes himself to believing in people so that they can also become who they aspire to be.

Dan had an advantage. He had a personal revelation of Coach God's presence during his sophomore year. I was Dan's confirmation sponsor. As we were sitting at Mass in St. Catherine's, the wind blew through Dan's hair. I was sitting right next to him but I didn't feel any breeze, as there was no draft or open doors. At the sign of peace, he turned to me and said, "Joe, you will never guess what happened!"

I replied, "Dan, shake their hands. You can tell me later."

I did not know what had happened until we talked out in the parking lot after the Mass. Once he told me of his experience, I recognized the indication of the presence of Coach God's Spirit, which often appeared as wind in the Scriptures. I told him he was fortunate to have such a sign of God's presence and love for him, but he might not want to tell his friends at school as they would think he was weird. This probably wasn't good advice because now I know that young people who believe in God are sometimes quiet about it. We don't share what we know deeply. We don't share miracles that happen to us out of humility or fear that no one would believe. Dan believed. He had been contacting me every year for thirty-five years to tell me stories of when he has been keenly aware of God's presence. He has been blessed.

We all have been blessed by that one person who believes in us. For some, it was our dad or our Mom. For others, it is an assistant coach. All of us are assistant coaches to the one who believes in us the most. Coach God believes in us more than we believe in Coach God. We can advocate for our sons, daughters, and players with Coach God, but think of the advocates we already have, Jesus, his mother. The Spirit was even called the advocate in the scriptures. How can we fail? We have the greatest group of assistant coaches ever assembled. Our head coach is the most forgiving of our mistakes and believes in us especially when we don't have the courage to believe in ourselves! So let us strengthen our drooping hands, *believe*, and get in the game! Our team depends on us to use sports as intended by our coach, Coach God!

There are ways we can allow Coach God to support us in a very intentional way. We all pray differently. In the history of Christian spirituality, these pathways may be speculative, but also kataphatic, apophatic, or affective. We also pray as unique individuals through our personal experiences. I cannot tell someone how to pray, one has to discover this for oneself. But Jesus can and did. In the Our Father, which unites our football team before games, I find everything I need to strengthen my weak knees. Even though this God is in heaven, I find God very present in the game on earth—or turf, if you will. In the Our Father, I can ask for what I need and still foster the spiritual serenity that comes with accepting God's will. Ultimately, I find myself humbled by the realization that I am imperfect and in need of forgiveness for my mistakes and sins.

Another conditioning exercise is our Sabbath observance. As a faithful Catholic, I celebrate the Eucharist on Saturday evenings or Sunday mornings. Youth practices on Sunday mornings put young athletes in a compromising position. Do they choose faith or sports? As I celebrate the Lenten season, I am reminded of the admonitions of the Prophet Isaiah that true fasting involves caring for the most vulnerable and seeking God on the Sabbath, not our own pleasure. Why do youth sports have to take place in the morning on Sundays if at all? They do not. A coach or community can dictate when practices happen as a way of instructing the players what they deem valuable in life. I often break down film on Sunday nights, correct papers, or plan lessons so I understand Coach Belichick's exhortation of "No days off!" during the New England Patriots' championship celebration at the Government Center in Boston. I also understand Nancy Frates' experience of faith and family and her holy endeavor of watching the children play as she gathers her flock on Sundays. This is not an either-or proposition for her. We need not choose either sports or spirituality. We need to achieve balance and wholeness to live holy lives. Nancy's Marian devotion, love of the mass, experience of sports, and devotion to her son Peter are all one body, all experiences of the body of Christ. For the nuns at Notre Dame who would pray their rosaries in the front row at Mass, their vocation was to pray for those in need, especially that poorly dressed man in the back row, Mark Bavaro. They used to pray that he would find a job. Little did they know that he would become a famous NFL player. His work on Sundays was an expression of his faith as surely as their praying the rosary was for them.

Last Sunday when I attended Mass, there was a banner that pleaded, "Open my eyes, Lord." As I came back from communion, I noticed Coach Tim O'Connor two pews ahead to my right. I had not recognized him previously. Tim was one of those players who lacked confidence as a starting underclass guard at St. Johns Prep. I will never forget the first quarter of an overtime win in our first ever game against a legendary Brockton program. Tim came over to the sidelines during the first time-out and said, "We can play with these guys."

We replied, "We told you that."

We believed in him until he believed in himself. So I boxed him in after Mass and asked him what he was doing there. He said that he and his wife discussed different houses of worship but he chose to remain Catholic. His grandmother used to bring him to Mass growing up. He celebrates the Eucharist every Sunday because it helps him achieve the peace he needs to be with his students and athletes in the way he wants to be with them. The way Coach God wants him to be with them. Tim was Division 1 Coach of the Year in Massachusetts this year, leading Haverhill High to its best record in decades. I heard numerous accounts of the great work he is doing with youth in his city. Although not awarded, I believe he is also Coach God's Assistant Coach of the Year. He helps his players believe in themselves by believing in them until they realize they are that good! By experiencing the very tangible presence of Coach O'Connor, his student and athletes are opened up to the real presence of the sacred mystery of God in our lives.

16

The Perfect Game

The *perfect game* is a baseball term associated with pitchers, not allowing a single hit or run. I played baseball up through freshman year of high school. Playing Little League was a big deal. Everyone played. All of the parents took it very seriously and lined the field with their lawn chairs, hanging on every pitch. I was always very nervous. I was nervous in sixth grade when the pitching got faster as I was afraid of getting hit. I was nervous that I was going to strike out whenever I was put in off of the bench, which I did more often than not. I was most nervous when a fly ball was hit to me in the outfield. I couldn't see it off the bat against a gray sky so if I caught the ball, it was a miracle. Little did I know that I needed to wear glasses. Due to my lazy eye, I overused one eye and had difficulty with depth perception. A perfect game was the furthest thing from my mind.

Because people in town knew I coached other sports at the varsity level in high school, they asked me to help coach my daughter's softball team and my son's baseball team. I took three years of studying the sport and picking the brain of the best coaches I knew before I felt confident to teach in Little League. I think this is common amongst parents who volunteer to coach. We want our children to play sports. We may have a little knowledge, but in my case, I often taught the wrong thing at the youth level. There were no clinics in those days for youth coaches. One passed on what one was taught, even if it was unwittingly the wrong thing. Coaching my daughter wasn't a problem. We spent a lot of quality time doing soft toss, batting, and fielding, and she had a great group of friends on her team. My son was a different story. He loved to be a catcher but was stuck out in right field. When he did get in, I could see his confidence dropping as he struggled at the plate. I felt helpless. Baseball is a game of statistics, and even at that level, some coaches make them public. This was devastating for my son. I hope he forgives me for doing what I thought was right by having him play baseball at a young age.

In high school, I actually played football for my dad. One of the worst moments came when as a tight end, I ran a seam pattern down the middle against Bishop Brady, and the quarterback dropped the ball right into my arms with great precision as I ran past the safety. I dropped the ball, and we were forced to punt. I will never forget running off the field by my father. He didn't say a word, just slowly shook his head, tight-lipped. The nervousness returned but I overcame it slightly and managed to catch a touchdown later in the game. I recently went back for a reunion of that team and no one remembered my dropped pass. They actually remembered me catching a lot more balls and touchdowns than I actually did, so I let them.

No one plays a perfect game, which makes it all the more difficult for those of us who are perfectionists to forgive ourselves for every little mistake. While others may remember the memorable good plays, we focus on what we did wrong. As a high school coach in New Hampshire, I remember one football player sitting on the steps after we had beaten a perennial powerhouse for the first time in school history. One could hear the singing and whooping it up in the locker room from outside. Shannon Fish was the quarterback who had led us to victory with his ball-handling, field leadership, and playing linebacker. He was sitting on the steps outside of the locker room, crying. I sat next to him and asked him why he wasn't inside celebrating with his friends. He focused on the one interception he had thrown. It could have cost us the game. He couldn't forgive himself. This is the beginning of forgiveness for others, recognizing that we are not perfect and being okay with that. From an early age, we put athletes in positions of pressure, some more than others. The point guard in basketball, quarterback and kicker in football, pitcher in baseball, and any goalie all are in the spotlight. The fans demand perfection even though they know the perfect game won't happen. So these young people heap unrealistic expectations on themselves then struggle to forgive themselves when they inevitably fail. My daughter came home from field hockey practice her sophomore year and said that the varsity coach and captains asked her to be the backup goalie. She told me she wouldn't do it, and I told her she would do whatever the coach asked of her unless it was unethical. Players don't get to choose their position, but coaches, players, and fans have the responsibility to forgive their magnified mistakes so that they can forgive themselves more easily. In this way, we are acting like Coach God. We hope for the same forgiveness from God and each other for our off-the-field offenses.

As a head coach in track and field and basketball, I made a lot of mistakes. I underestimated talent. For my last game as a varsity head basketball coach, I started senior Dan Mullen, the current University of Florida head football coach, for the first time, and he scored eighteen points. On the way to the bus, I walked alongside him and said, "I'm sorry, Dan. I should have played you more." He said, "That's okay, Coach. I forgive you." I will never forget that moment. I thought I was a pretty good coach but I became aware of some of my failings, such as losing people on the bench. That's why assistant coaches help with making suggestions because the head coach is so busy with game adjustments in the fast pace of the game that a player can get lost and not play as much as they should, if only the head coach listens. I don't think I was the best listener, and I still need forgiveness for that. In basketball, everyone thinks they should be playing more, and at least one player actually playing thinks they should be getting the ball more. We cannot keep everyone or their families happy. All the more remarkable that a young Dan Mullen forgave me because I'm certain there were others who did not. That stayed with me all of these years, and I'm forever indebted to him for his forgiveness. As a coach, he continues helping young men today to be the best people they can be while coaching at a very high level. But at that moment, he was already coaching at a high level. He was ending his career as a player and coaching me as Coach God would, forgiving my imperfections.

Many of my failures in this book come from boy's athletics, though I also coached girls' basketball, softball, and track and field. Maybe it is because the girls and young women I coached were more overtly grateful for anything I taught them. That is why I like the image of Coach God as a woman, like the woman looking for the lost coin in Luke's gospel. I still hear from one of them every Christmas. Heather, Shannon's sister, had every reason not to forgive me. I have been a finalist for a head coaching basketball job several times. During Heather's high school career, I was a finalist for the boys' basketball job together with a coach from the Bronx. He got the job so the athletic committee offered me the vacant girls' job. I assisted that program during the previous year so I took the job. Two weeks later, a member of the board came out to the football field and told me that the coach from the Bronx reneged and they wanted me to be the head coach of the boys' program. I accepted. It wasn't right. I became part of the problem of the ongoing struggle for equality in women's sports. I should have stuck with my original commitment and honored the young women I had previously coached. Maybe there are some girls from that team that don't forgive me, and I'm sure there are some readers who are upset with my choice. What a terrible message to those young women! I'm fortunate Heather forgave me and still offers me her love and friendship. I only hope for such mercy from Coach God.

Coaching track and field in Manchester, New Hampshire, was life-giving. All four high schools used the same track every day. We cooperated on lane and facility utilization and even coached each other's athletes if we had more expertise in that area. There was no ego. Everything was for the success of the athletes. One day, I was coaching various shot putters and heard my name being yelled across the field. I ran over to the pole vault pit and found Charlie sitting against the mat with blood running out of his nose and ears. There were no pay phones handy so I drove him to the hospital myself with one of my captains trying to hold his head steady in the back seat. This was stupid, I know. It was not a perfect game plan. It turns out he had a skull fracture six inches vertically in the back of his head and some hearing loss. The next day, his mother called me up. She asked, "Coach Lovett, what are the legal dimensions of the pole vault mats?" I replied, "It doesn't matter. Charlie and his friend only took out two of the required mats. When his friend tried to teach him pole vault, he went up on the pole, turned sideways, and fell, hitting his head on the concrete. If they pulled out all three mats, he would have landed safely." She thanked me for my honesty. I didn't hear from her until the following year when Charlie ran track again his senior year. She called me to remind me that Charlie should not pole vault. Charlie and I agreed. Even though I was put in an impossible position coaching over eighty boys and girls by myself and could not be everywhere on the track, I was still responsible for Charlie's health. She forgave me. My life would have been much different if she did not. Thank God!

As a player, parent, and coach, I have been in need of forgiveness and fortunate that some of the people in my life extended it to me. Fans also need to forgive. Many players have been "crucified" by fans for missing field goals, missing free throws, or dropping balls. We, as the fans who may have idolized them, have failed to forgive them for mistakes of technique, not even sins! Yet we hope for the forgiveness from Coach God for our very real failings. If we truly see ourselves as part of a team, the sixth or tenth or twelfth man so to speak, we need to forgive as those teammates and coaches forgive us. They all understand we do not play a perfect game, neither do they play or coach a perfect game. An account of my own individual failures could go on for many more pages. If we like to see ourselves as part of a *nation* or *family*, we need to forgive on a daily basis, as we do in family life. What family can survive without mercy and forgiveness? This is how Coach God wants us to be fans. He knows a little bit about being a fan. God is our biggest fan, always wanting us to be our best, hoping for our perfect game, and giving us a boost at those critical moments of our life. But when we fail, Coach God picks us up and encourages us to try again. That is why I like the penitential rite at the Catholic mass. Every week, I acknowledge my sins and ask my fellow players to forgive me and pray for me. I will never be perfect. No one is, except God. As we strive to be more like God, let us also be like God in forgiving each other from the heart. Now that would truly be a good sport!

17

Stretching: the Truth

On July 27, 1993, Reggie Lewis died in Waltham, Massachusetts. I was in Waltham that week, working as a basketball coach at the Bentley College overnight basketball camp. As the shocking news spread, I was asked to break the news to the players. One of my jobs was to lead the stretching for all three hundred athletes in the field house each morning. So after the stretch, I gathered them all in, told them the terrible news, and then sent them off to their station work. Thankfully, another coach, Uylen Coleman, stopped them, called them back in, sat them down, and spent about ten minutes *really* explaining the impact of his death not only on his family and the Celtics organization, but also on the African-American community. I had no idea. I was—and am—an ignorant man. I had no idea of the impact Reggie Lewis had on communities like Roxbury where the center stands in his name. I had announced his death but not honored his life. A few years ago, when was my son was playing basketball for St. John's Prep and his son was playing for Catholic Memorial, I sought Ulyen out in the stands, reintroduced myself, and thanked him. I'm sure he was angry at my ignorance that day in 1993, but he accepted my thanks and apology.

In writing this book, I have been blessed with the personal experiences and deeply held spiritual beliefs of many people. I hope I have been a good listener and honored their lives more fully than I honored the life of Reggie Lewis. What I thought I was going to write was not actually what I ended up writing, and I am happy about that. If I were to write a book about being open to the spirit of Coach God and all of the many ways God reveals to us about spirituality through sports but remained closed myself, then the book should remain closed, even unpublished. Still, I know there are unresolved conflicts and difficulties with what I have written. I'm not sure if I will address them in future books, but I know they exist. My book is explicitly Catholic and unashamedly professes belief in Jesus Christ. This is who I am and it's part of my identity, but I am also a Holocaust Legacy Partner. After giving one witness talk retelling the story of Jack Kornhauser, a middle school student told my son, "I didn't know your father is Jewish." I am Catholic, but in that moment, I knew I honored Jack's story. I believe that all religions are meant to be one while acknowledging our differences. We all need to accept that unifying principle that was a hallmark of the founding of America, the sovereignty of God, no matter what religion we profess. We should practice our religion as an expression of our faith while looking for ways to share our common beliefs. Sports help us share our spiritual lives. We are all on Coach God's team. I am honored that as of this writing, a Hindu man is considering designing the cover and a Jewish man is helping me publish the book. They know I am Catholic and accept me for who I am, as I accept them. This is critical in a world rife with the ignorance that resists the facts and leads to ethno-religious hatred. No one group has a monopoly on the truths about God's love for us. We need to stretch the truth to include us all.

Suffering is unique to everyone. We all experience our own pain and suffering. I first entered into the mystery of suffering when my three-year-old family friend Emily suffered irreparable brain damage from her poncho getting tangled in a swing set. For a year, eight different people went out to that house every day to try to reestablish her neurological pathways. We were from eleven different faith communities but we came together as part of God's team to help Emily. Every faith community took a different month to provide supper for the family so they could be more present to Emily during that first year. I don't know why Emily suffered then or still suffers now. I just live with the mystery. When my two-year-old-niece Clare died of leukemia, I could not pray for a year. The only prayer that made sense was, "Lord, have mercy." So I do not presume how one should pray. I have only offered the insights I have gained. My learning has not stopped. As I put the final period on the "When Bad Things Happen to Good Players" chapter, the phone rang. My mother-in-law's heart stopped during a procedure. She was revived but plunged into deeper suffering, and we all continue to journey into that mystery with her. While riding on the bus to the Shriner's hospital to visit burned and crippled children as part of the 1978 New Hampshire Shrine team, I was sitting on the bus next to Portsmouth's Dwight "Hambone" Hamsley. We ended up having a deep religious discussion. During the course of the bus ride, we heard the announcement over the radio that Pope John Paul I died. We shared that historic moment. One week later, we shared another. That year, Dwight broke the Shrine game rushing record with over two hundred yards. The next year while on vacation in Hawaii, he was up in a tree reading a Bible and fell. He became paralyzed. Why did that happen? I don't claim to know nor do I claim to know the unique meaning of anyone else's suffering. But I don't believe it is meaningless. I do believe God is with us.

I am ignorant of the experiences of Latino Catholics. I believe their experiences are different that my experiences as a privileged white male. They know truths about Coach God that I have yet to learn. My colleague Raisa has told me of how the church community welcomed her and supported her when she came to this country as an immigrant. It became her spiritual home in an environment that was sometimes hostile outside of the faith. I need to do a better job at welcoming the stranger in my communities and to listen to the stories of others instead of focusing on my own story.

Professional sports in America is big business. How can this reconcile with a preferential option for the poor? I am reminded of Matthew's assertion, "Blessed are the poor in spirit." We all are dependent upon God. So many professional athletes are thankful for their blessings and give back to their communities as Reggie Lewis did and as Pat Connaughton does with his With Us foundation. There are no cuts on Coach God's team based on wealth, but there are also no ways to buy a position on the team. God stretches the truth of God's love to include all of us if we have the humility to be open to accepting it.

This book is mostly about male athletes because that is most of my experience. I am aware that there are female football players, like former student Kelly Dobbins who played a tackle in women's arena football or Carly who played in AAU basketball for me and was also a quarterback in her middle school. Maureen McAleer was our first varsity rugby coach at St. John's. They are all strong, independent women. So were the mothers I wrote about, Nancy Frates and Dawn Coppola. There is no singular way to express the image of God as a woman. This is a theological concept that needs further exploration if we are to fully realize the many ways God reveals to us and coaches us through the women in our lives. I have witnessed the courage of athletes confronting coaches who make demeaning comments about girls or sexual orientation. I am thankful I have lived long enough to see hostility toward anyone who is considered different abated and teammates and coaches accepted for whom they are. A lot of us have stretched the truth as we have learned it in this regard and so I have not included any anecdotes regarding this in the book. Instead, I want to encourage everyone to accept people as they are, as Coach God does. There is still work to be done in this area. Programs like "If you can play, you can play" help us focus on the truth that Coach God wants all of his sons and daughters to experience all that sports can bring to our lives, regardless of sexual orientation.

In the end, sports and religion are not an either-or proposition. In a rowboat, if one only uses either oar, one moves in a circle, going nowhere. To move forward, both our religious practices and our experiences as coaches, players, parents, and fans in sports should nurture our spiritual life, strengthen our faith, and remind us that Coach God is always with us and loving us. In the movie, *Greater*, the high school coach often asked his team, "Have I told you lately that I love you?" I have written about my experiences with the truth, my spiritual insights. My hope is that one can stretch that truth to include one's own and others. As for me, to quote my mother-in-law Carol Christian LaPointe, "That's my story and I'm sticking to it."

CONCLUSION
PLAYING TIME

W hen I was a sophomore in high school, I had a class entitled, Dead is a Four-Letter Word. The teacher, Mrs. Poore, asked us to write down something we wanted to do before we die. As a public school student, I didn't have much religious education. As a bit of a wise guy, I spent most of my time in parish religion class fooling around. I wrote, "Read the Bible." I still can see her cursive red words in the margin of my yellow notebook paper. She wrote, "It is never too late to start." I started that night reading ten chapters a night. By the end of sophomore year, I had read the entire Bible from cover to cover. Everything in the Bible told me I had to work with the poor so I decided I should become a priest. Through five years of study and discernment, I realized that I was called instead to be a teacher and coach, which is the position Coach God wanted me to play.

I am glad I work at a Xaverian Brothers Sponsored School whose mission is to include all people but is especially called to reach out to the poor and marginalized. I often struggle with a potential conflict between the gospel of poverty and a gospel of prosperity. This is a historic struggle as the American Catholic Church moved from an immigrant community to success for the affluent. Currently the Church is in flux again as a vibrant Latino church lives the gospel by welcoming all people and supporting them in difficult journeys. I believe in this historical time period, we are called to embrace both the devout poor of God and the poor in spirit who recognize one's complete dependence upon God regardless of economic status. Our sporting lives can become all about us if we let them take over our lives. An attitude of "What can I get?" can replace servant leadership, humility, and giving what we have received as a gift.

The gift we have been given is playing time. Questions about playing time are those most often asked of coaches if players and their parents focus on the external goods of athletics instead of the spiritual benefits of sports and play. Some coaches won't even address questions of playing time. They feel the player and parent have no right to question the coach. They should trust the coach's judgment, integrity, and expertise. Questions of playing time can detract from the team's overall goals, however ill- or well-defined the coach made those goals. With Coach God, questions of playing time and questions in general are radically different! Coach God asks the questions like, "Do you want to be well?" and "Who do you say that I am?" and "What are you looking for?" I think Jesus understood that our mind operates on the principle of questions. Even when we are not consciously thinking of the answers, our mind is searching for them. The wisest people don't give us the smart answers; they know how to invite us into the questions. This is what Jesus did with his parables. He invites us to delve more deeply into the mystery of our relationships with Coach God and our teammates, meaning everyone.

God's team goals are clear: to know, love, and serve God and to live in loving community with God and others forever! Moreover, Coach God gives us all equal playing time in giving us life. We don't all live to the same age, but we are all always playing by living. This gift of our life and the questions God asks of us are the foundation for a sound spiritual life lived through sports. We did not earn our spot in life. Through the mystery of our life in the community as a member of Coach God's team, we can live with the mystery and extend Coach God's game plan to include all of us all of the time. We don't all get a medal. As a matter of fact, none of us do. But in the end, we all win. Amen to that!

ABOUT THE AUTHOR

Joseph grew up on the sidelines in Vermont and New Hampshire, watching his father, Tom Lovett, coach multiple sports with dedication and integrity. After excelling in football, basketball, and track and field in high school, he accepted an academic scholarship from Providence College, receiving his BA (1992) and MA (1993) in theology.

He first began teaching religious studies in 1983 at Trinity High School in New Hampshire where he also served as department chair. He was the inaugural God and Youth winner for the Diocese of Manchester for his outstanding service to youth in New Hampshire. At Trinity, Joe served as assistant basketball coach from 1983–1985, winning the state Division 1 title in 1985. He later served as head coach from 1987–1989. Coach Lovett was an assistant football coach from 1983–1987 and head track and field coach for both boys and girls in 1983–1990. Coach Lovett left Trinity High School in 1990 to accept a position as religious studies teacher and campus minister at St. John's Preparatory School in Danvers, Massachusetts. He was given the Ryken Award in 2004. This award is presented annually to a member of an XBSS school who proclaims the Gospel of Jesus Christ, enriches the faith of others, pursues academic excellence, and strives to fulfill the gospel call to justice and peace. During his tenure at St. John's, he has served as assistant football coach (1990–present), assistant track and field coach (1993–2000), and assistant basketball coach (1990–1992, 1996–2013). His teams won state titles in football (1997, 2002) and basketball (2011), as well as numerous Catholic Conferences championships. He was also the director of intramural and recreational sports and is currently the camp director for Camp Christopher, having served as assistant director for twenty-six summers.

He has been married to his wife Diane for twenty-six years. They have two grown children, Sean (Bates College 2018) and Jennifer (Wheaton College 2020), both are college athletes. As a parent, Coach Lovett volunteered in coaching youth basketball, baseball, softball, and AAU basketball for a total of seventeen additional seasons. He had the good fortune of coaching numerous high school athletes who later achieved success as professional and Olympic athletes.

CPSIA information can be obtained
at www.ICGtesting.com
Printed in the USA
LVHW04s1221030918
588991LV00003B/22/P